Please return/renew this item
by the last date shown.
Books may also be renewed by
phone or the Internet.

Tel: 0161 217 6009
www.stockport.gov.uk/libraries

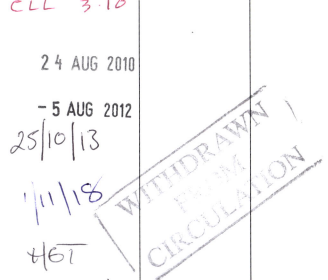

David Horner
David Madgett

Series editor

Tim Chapman

es

Published in 2009 by:
Nelson Thornes Ltd
Delta Place
27 Bath Road
CHELTENHAM
GL53 7TH
United Kingdom

09 10 11 12 13 / 10 9 8 7 6 5 4 3 2 1

A catalogue record for this book is available from the British Library

ISBN 978 1 4085 0434 5

Cover photograph by Corbis/Simon Marcus
Illustrations by eMC Design Ltd
Page make-up by eMC Design Ltd

Printed and bound in Spain by GraphyCems

Contents

Acknowledgements

The authors and publisher would like to thank the following for permission to reproduce photographs and other copyright material:

Text

P14 Reducing package sizes/raising prices adapted from article in New York Times; p19 AER statements adapted from www.investorprofit.com - reprinted with permission; p25 Ethical lending policy statement from www.equator-principles.com; p10 Benefits and financial support from www.direct.gov.uk © Crown Copyright reprinted under Crown Copyright PSI License C2008002303.

P30 Case study table on employment numbers © Crown Copyright reprinted under Crown Copyright PSI License 2008002303:p31 Internet v TV advertising adapted from www.guardian.co.uk; p36 Educational achievement by ethnic origin from www.statistics.gov.uk © Crown Copyright reprinted under Crown Copyright PSI License C2008002303; p37 Case study benefits table from Dept for Work and Pensions © Crown Copyright reprinted under Crown Copyright PSI License C2008002303; p38 Case study average pay from www.statistics.gov.uk © Crown Copyright reprinted under Crown Copyright PSI License C2008002303;p39 Case study skills shortages from © Crown Copyright reprinted under Crown Copyright PSI License C2008002303; p41 Case study unemployment rates from www.statistics.gov.uk © Crown Copyright reprinted under Crown Copyright PSI License C2008002303.

P46-7 Balance of payment table from © Crown Copyright reprinted under Crown Copyright PSI License C2008002303; p48 Case study on global trade figures from British Council report 'Global Value – The Value of UK Education and Training © Crown Copyright reprinted under Crown Copyright PSI License C2008002303.Exports', Sept 2007; p49 CO_2 emission sources adapted from Carbon Trust website; p49 Case study on roses from Cranfield University, Williams, 2007; p50 Quotation on exchange rates from www.belfasttelegraph.co.uk; p51 Quotation on weak sterling from www.fwi.co.uk; p54 M&S moving offshore quote from Adapted from http://news.bbc.co.uk/1/hi/business/1806463.stm; p54 Pat Conroy quote adapted from www.marketingcharts.com; p55 Fairtrade logo reproduced with permission; p56 Sainsbury's quote adapted from http://news.bbc.co.uk/1/hi/business/4316207.stm; p56 Sweatshop text adapted from: http://elektric-kat.blogspot.com/2005/03/why-we-should-boycott-sweatshop-labour.html; p57 Case study on sweatshops adapted from: http://findarticles.com/p/articles/mi_qa5378/is_/ai_n21478788; p58 Case study on offshore manufacturing adapted from http://news.bbc.co.uk; p58 M&S offshore manufacturing adapted from http://news.bbc.co.uk; p59 Peugeot statement adapted from http://news.bbc.co.uk; p60 Case study text on TVR adapted from http://news.bbc.co.uk; p61 Case study on migrant employment from www.fastfoodjobs.co.uk. p61 SAWS case study from www.workpermit.com; p61 Case study deal with Belgium adapted from http://news.bbc.co.uk.

P65 UK key economic statistics from www.statistics.gov.uk © Crown Copyright reprinted under Crown Copyright PSI License C2008002303; p67 Income inequality in the UK from www.statistics.gov.uk © Crown Copyright reprinted under Crown Copyright PSI License C2008002303 p67 UK economic growth 2003–8 from www.statistics.gov.uk © Crown Copyright reprinted under Crown Copyright PSI License C2008002303; p69 Percentage of population living below 60% of median income from Luxembourg income study; p77 www.statistics.gov.uk © Crown Copyright reprinted under Crown Copyright PSI License C2008002303 p77 2007 Pre-Budget Report and Comprehensive Spending Review October 2007 www.hm-treasury.gov.uk/pbr_csr07_repindex.htm © Crown Copyright reprinted under Crown Copyright PSI License C2008002303; p80 Interest rates March 2006 - November 2008 from www.statistics.gov.uk © Crown Copyright reprinted under Crown Copyright PSI License C2008002303; p85 Exchange rate for the pound against the euro from www.economist.com.

P90 Band of England bank rate since 1991 adapted from www.bbc.co.uk; p91 graphs adapted from www.bbc.co.uk.

Photos

P7 and banner, Alamy/Keith Morris; p8 case study photo of Nathan author's own; p10 student iStockphoto, couple with new house Alamy/Image Source Pink, young family Alamy/Simon Barber, cycling couple Photolibrary/Barrow Scott, bowling couple Alamy/ Photolocation Ltd; p11 Alamy/David Levenson; p12 girls shopping Alamy/Steve Hamblin, teenage outing Alamy/Photodisc; p13 people carrier Mitsubishi, kitchen Ikea; p15 refuelling Alamy/Bjanka Kadic, loading bananas Alamy/Travelshots.com; p16 wedding group Alamy/DigitalVision, window shopping Alamy/Kirsty McLaren, penny jar Alamy/studiomode; p17 Alamy/ICP; p18 young gamers Alamy/Dan Atkin, university students Alamy/William Robinson; p19 www.which4u.co.uk; p20 gold vending machine TG Gold-Super-Markt, Reijo author's own; p21 Alamy/vario images GmbH & Co.KG; p23 dream flat Alamy/View Pictures Ltd, plane ticket Istockphoto, sports car Alamy./izmostock.

P27 and banner, Fotolia; p29 student iStockphoto, house parent Alamy/ Nick Kennedy, retired couple iStockphoto; p31 Rex Features/Alex Segre; p33 factory workers Alamy/Jupiterimages/Brand X; desirable company car Honda; p34 multi payslips Alamy/Rosemary Roberts, McGonagle's payslip www.moneysoft.co.uk; p35 Getty Images; p40 Jobcentreplus Alamy/ Peter Scholey, job seeker Rex Features/Jonathan Banks; p41 Alamy/Simon Rawles; p42 quality childcare Alamy./Janine Wiedel Photolibrary, New Deal Alamy/Photodisc; p43 Alamy/vario images GmbH & Co.KG.

P45 and banner, iStockphoto; p46 grocery basket, coffee beans and banks, all iStockphoto, aeroplanes Alamy/Andrew Butterton; p48 holidays Alamy/ Art Kowalsky, food and light bulb iStockphoto; p49 carbon footprint Alamy/Mark Boulton, rose farming Still Pictures/Jorgen Schytte; p50 Alamy/Keith Erskine; p51 iStockphoto; p52 coke The Coca-Cola Company, suncream Alamy/ Greg Balfour Evans; p53 champagne Alamy/Pick and Mix Images, Audi car Alamy/ Tom Wood; p54 St Martin's School, richinfairness.com; p55 label with permission of Fairtrade, landed bluefin and tuna steak both Photolibrary; p56 working child Alamy/ Jacques Jangoux, protesters Still Pictures; p57 factory Still Pictures Joerg Boethling, class in Somalia courtesy of Department for International Development; p59 The Body Shop; p60 Alamy/Jim Nicholson.

P63 and banner iStockphoto; p64 Alamy/Alex Segre; p65 Alamy/Aardvark; p66 Alamy/ David Noton Photography; p68 iStockphoto; p69 Salvation Army; p70 Science Photo Library/CNRI; p71 Alamy/Andrew Fox; p74 Woolworths Alamy/Martin Jenkinson, shop closures Alamy/Chris Howes/Wild Places Photography; p75 Alamy/Paul Doyle; p76 iStockphoto; p78 by permission from The Guardian; p81 Alamy/Mike Booth; p83 iStockphoto; p84 Alamy/Mike Booth; p85 euros Istockphoto, European Central Bank Alamy/Datacraft Co. Ltd.

P88 Fotolia.

Every effort to obtain permission has been made, and any omissions will be rectified at reprinting.

Nelson Thornes has worked in partnership with AQA to make sure that this book offers you the best possible support for your GCSE course. All the content has been approved by the senior examining team at AQA, so you can be sure that it gives you just what you need when you are preparing for your exams.

■ How to use this book

This book covers everything you need for your course.

Learning Objectives

At the beginning of each section or topic you'll find a list of Learning Objectives based on the requirements of the specification, so you can make sure you are covering everything you need to know for the exam.

Objectives

Objectives

Objectives

Objectives

First objectives.

Second objective.

AQA Examiner's Tips

Don't forget to look at the AQA Examiner's Tips throughout the book to help you with your study and prepare for your exam.

AQA Examiner's tip

Don't forget to look at the AQA Examiner's Tips throughout the book to help you with your study and prepare for your exam.

AQA Examination-style Questions

These offer opportunities to practise doing questions in the style that you can expect in your exam so that you can be fully prepared on the day. Examination-style questions are reproduced with permission of the Assessment and Qualifications Alliance.

Visit **www.nelsonthornes.com/aqagcse** for more information.

GCSE Economics

■ What is Economics?

Economics is about making sense of your life! A huge range of choices and uncertainties face you every day. With an income you probably feel is too limited, what do you really want to buy? How will your holiday money be affected by a change in the exchange rate? What should you look for in a career? Some of these questions are serious, some not, but they all impact on your life – and not your life alone, but on the lives of others as well. A simple decision to buy a Fairtrade product, for example, has implications well beyond where you live, and even beyond the UK. What you buy can make the difference between extreme poverty and a sustainable life for a Third World farmer. The brand of clothes you wear could send a message that will help stop businesses exploiting child labour. Thinking hard about the energy consumption of your new computer before you buy could help reduce global warming. 'Personal economics' is about understanding the issues behind the choices you make.

Studying AQA Economics at GCSE level involves exploring these issues in two ways. Firstly it looks at personal economics:

- how we handle money and make decisions with limited incomes
- the purpose, nature and rewards of work, and what it means to be unemployed
- the impact of trading goods and services internationally
- how changes in the exchange rate impact the economy and personal decisions
- how the global economy affects the world of work.

Secondly it looks at how the economy is managed from the perspective of governments:

- the government's economic goals
- how the economy works
- how and why governments try to control the economy
- the influence of the EU on the UK economy.

GCSE Economics involves investigating all these aspects, and more, through applying economic ideas to real life situations. Using the tools and insights of Economics helps you look at the facts from different angles, to explain why things happen in the way they do. It even enables you to predict what might happen in the future. It helps you make choices by thinking things through, using reasoned judgements to make informed decisions.

■ What is the book about?

As you will want a really good Economics GCSE grade, this book is written to help you achieve exactly that. It is a student's book, designed to provide you with concise and clear explanations for each topic. We've included frequent key terms and 'Examiner's Tips', so you can learn to think just like the examiner. There are also lots of interesting real life case studies and examples to support your learning. On every page there are activities as well, helping to stimulate and develop your understanding.

The book is divided into five chapters. The first three chapters prepare you for the AQA Economics GCSE short course – Unit 11, Personal economics. These cover:

- money
- work
- the national and global economy.

You will be assessed on one written paper of 1¼ hours worth 100% of the marks for the short course; if you are completing the full course this will be worth 50% of your marks.

The final two chapters cover the specification for the remaining part of the AQA full GCSE – Unit 12, Investigating economic issues:

- investigating economic isues
- current economic issues.

You will be assessed by a further written paper of 1¼ hours, worth 50% of your total marks.

In addition, examination-style questions are provided at the end of the book, to help you practise the examination skills you will need.

1 Money

Aims

✔ Understand the personal life cycle – how people's needs for spending, saving and borrowing change at key points in life.

✔ Understand demand – how people's needs and wants change at key points in the personal life cycle.

✔ Understand why prices change – how the decisions of buyers and competing businesses affect prices in the market.

✔ Understand how and why people save money and that potential rewards from savings reflect the degree of risk involved.

✔ Understand the different methods of borrowing and how the interest rates charged reflect the type of loan.

✔ Understand why financial planning is necessary and how budgeting helps in managing money.

Trying to decide what to buy is a problem for everyone because incomes are limited but wants are not. Although these decisions change as people grow older, they don't go away! This chapter looks at how people satisfy their needs and wants over their lifetime by buying goods and services, and at the choices they have to make when deciding what to buy. We look at how businesses compete for people's money and how competition can affect both the prices we pay and the quality of the goods we buy.

Buying expensive items may mean that people need to save or borrow money. This chapter looks at the variety of methods of both saving and borrowing available. It also considers what people need to take into account before making a decision on which methods to use. Sometimes, the government helps people manage their money if they are poor or vulnerable in some way (e.g. students or pensioners). Managing money is one of the most important and fundamental life skills, and this chapter looks at the basic principles involved.

Understanding the personal life cycle

The personal life cycle

Most people will experience leaving home, working, establishing their own families and retiring. This is known as the personal life cycle. Throughout this progression, **incomes** will change significantly: firstly when someone gets a job, and then as they advance their career. Retirement is likely to see income fall again.

Needs (those things people need to have to survive (e.g. water and heating)) and wants (the things that make life more enjoyable) also change as circumstances change. At all stages of life, most people's income will be limited compared with their needs and certainly their wants, and they will have to make decisions. For each choice there is an opportunity cost (see 1.2 Making decisions). People may have to pay for university course fees, rent and so on, and will need to carefully weigh the benefits they expect to receive in potential higher future salary against these.

Later, people may want to buy rather than rent a house, so they may need to **borrow** large amounts of money. Once children leave home, people may have more disposable income and therefore will be able to save money for retirement. On retirement, they may need to use up some **savings** to supplement their pension.

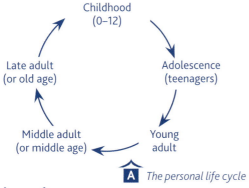

A *The personal life cycle*

Needs and wants

Understand the idea of a personal life cycle and the different stages within it.

Understand the difference between 'needs' and 'wants' and how these change over the personal life cycle.

Understand how changes in income affect an individual's decisions.

Understand that opportunity costs will arise, due to decisions.

Understand how governments affect a person's income and expenditure.

Key terms

Income: total money received from a person's wages/salary, interest and dividends.

Borrowing: getting money from a lender that must be repaid in the future (e.g. a mortgage).

Savings: putting money aside for later use.

Case study

Nathan is a successful public relations (PR) consultant, thanks to an outgoing personality and sharp intelligence. At 35, he is near the height of his earnings potential, at around £100,000+ per year. He started his career with a student loan of £8000. The interest on this loan was subsidised by the government, but his starting salary was also low. Ten years ago, he and his partner, Tracy, wanted to buy a £75,000 house in Norwich, and this meant borrowing money for a mortgage of £65,000 and using Tracy's savings of £10,000.

As Nathan's children were growing up, he received several promotions but has now left his firm to become a freelance PR consultant, and his income has greatly increased.

He is developing an expensive taste for tailor-made suits, on the grounds of the image he needs to portray to clients. He is also weighing up the costs and benefits of buying a new 'people-carrier' vehicle for his family.

At all stages of the personal life cycle, incomes are likely to be limited. They are a 'scarce resource'. Needs and wants, however, are likely to be unlimited. People have to decide between the purchases that are essential (needs) and those that are not (wants). Whether something is a need or want depends on the circumstances. A mobile phone is a 'need' for a busy business person, but arguably a 'want' for a teenager.

■ Changes in income

Case study

On leaving university, Nathan changed from spending money on parties to buying a house. His first house was very limited by what he could afford on a starting salary. As he got promotions, he could afford a wider selection of properties, more expensive holidays, clothes, and so on.

Activities

1. In small groups, make lists of things that you consider to be 'wants' for a teenager and those you think are 'needs'.

2. Explain whether Nathan's habit of buying tailor-made suits is a 'need' or a 'want'.

3. If Nathan goes on to become a millionaire, how might his 'needs' and 'wants' change?

Key terms

Needs and wants: needs are essential to our lives but wants are things we could survive without.

Leaving school, college/university: when a person ceases to be in full-time education and looks for employment.

Gaining employment: being offered and accepting a paid job.

Promotion: a new higher-paid job role involving greater responsibility and skill.

Debt: the amount still owing from funds borrowed.

Unemployment: when an individual without a job is seeking paid employment or is able to work.

■ Key milestones in the personal life cycle

Important events ('milestones') in the personal life cycle will affect our finances. Typical milestones are likely to include:

Leaving school: The point at which someone stops being looked after 24/7 by their parents and starts managing their own life. They then either go on to further education or find a job. Gaining higher qualifications is expensive but can help a person earn more in later life.

Gaining employment: If someone is successful in gaining qualifications, they will have a wider choice of jobs. The higher the level of qualification, the more likely they are to find a better-paid job, but they may have to choose between higher pay or a job that is more enjoyable and satisfying.

Promotion: If people work hard and are responsible, they may be promoted or find better-paid employment. This is called promotion. Promotion gives people the opportunity to develop skills, but it also allows them to take on greater financial commitments and buy more goods and services. Depending on the point in their career, it may also enable them to build up savings or pay off debts.

Unemployment: If someone loses their job for some reason, they become unemployed. An unemployed person may need financial help from the government as they will no longer receive a wage or salary. Benefits paid by the government can help in these circumstances. If we have built up savings, these may now have to be used to support our lifestyle while we seek further employment.

Retirement: When people reach the age of 60 (for women – rising to 65 in 2020) or 65 (for men), they reach the official retirement age. They can now cease paid work because they will receive a state pension, and possibly an additional pension from their employer. A person with a private pension or adequate savings can choose to stop work voluntarily at any time. Savings decisions made earlier in life will help determine how much money someone can spend in retirement. Post-retirement income is likely to be lower than income earned from work, so difficult adjustments may have to be made to lifestyles.

B *Milestones many of us hope to reach: studying, buying a home, raising a family, active middle age and active retirement.*

Nathan's mother, Abigail, has had a successful career as a midwife. However, as she approaches retirement she has decided to cut down on work to spend more time helping to look after her grandchildren. Over the last few years, Abigail has been able to put aside quite a lot of money which she hopes to use to supplement her pension when she reaches 60.

Activities

4 Why might Abigail have been able to save money in the years before she retired?

5 How are Abigail's spending needs likely to change as she enters retirement?

Activities

6 Why did Nathan need to borrow money when he started out on his career?

7 Describe how Nathan's financial situation is likely to change as he progresses along his personal life cycle. Explain your reasons carefully.

How the government affects stages of the personal life cycle

There are many points in people's lives when they may need additional financial help from the government. This is provided through the **benefits** system.

❝ *The benefits system provides practical help and financial support if you are unemployed and looking for work. It also provides you with additional income when your earnings are low, if you are bringing up children, are retired, care for someone, are ill or have a disability.* ❞

Source: Benefits and financial support www.direct.gov.uk

Key terms

Retirement: when we cease to do paid employment.

Benefits: regular payments from a government to support people in need.

AQA Examiner's tip

You need to explain clearly how a person's income and expenditure could be affected by any one of these milestones.

For those aged 16–19, the government pays an Education Maintenance Allowance of £10–£30 per week to encourage pupils from poorer families to continue their education. Money can also be provided for child care to those under 20 who want to continue their studies. For those going on to university, the government subsidises the course fees and provides low-interest 'student loans'. The rates of interest charged on student loans are low compared with a bank loan.

For people of working age, there are benefits to help them find or maintain employment. **Tax credits** help increase the take-home income of low-paid workers, so they are better off working rather than claiming unemployment benefits. The tax credit reduces the income tax they have to pay.

Jobcentre Plus offices provide benefits and services to help people to find work (Jobseeker's Allowance), start up their own business, help individuals manage in low-paid jobs or help with work-related accidents or illness.

The government pays **pensions** to people in retirement if they have paid sufficient National Insurance contributions. A pension is vital because most people over 65 will no longer get an income from work. The government also pays a variety of other benefits to pensioners on low incomes (e.g. the winter fuel payment, currently between £250 and £400 each year).

Activity

8 Carry out some research to find out other ways that the government helps a those in retirement b the unemployed. You may like to start by looking at the government's own website **www.direct.gov.uk**

Case study

Nathan's grandfather, now in his 80s, needs a regular home-help to help with household tasks. The government gives him a care assistant's allowance for this, which helps towards the cost.

In order to pay for these benefits, the government collects **taxes**. One of the main taxes is income tax (also known as Pay As You Earn or PAYE). The amount of income tax you pay is related to how much you earn. In 2009, the basic rate of income tax is 20 per cent but higher earners pay 40 per cent on anything they earn over £34,800.

The personal **tax allowance** means that a UK citizen in 2009 can earn up to £6,035 without having to pay any income tax. Pensioners receive higher age-related personal allowances – up to £9,180 for persons aged 75 or over.

On 24 November 2008, the Chancellor of the Exchequer announced several tax changes to help families cope with the recession. Jim Murphy, the Scottish Secretary, said, 'This means the average Scottish family will be better off. It will see a £600 increase in the personal income tax allowance … with a further rise in the future, as well as increases in Child Benefit and the basic state pension.'

Case study

C

Activities

9 Who would benefit from the increase in the personal tax allowance?

10 Explain how the age-related income tax allowance would influence the purchases of a typical pensioner.

11 Explain how a family's spending habits are likely to change as a result of the £600 increase in the income tax allowance.

1.2 Making decisions

■ Decision-making and opportunity costs

Scarcity and the basic economic problem

As a result of **scarcity,** everyone has to make **choices**. We all face the **basic economic problem** that our needs and wants are infinite but **resources** and incomes are scarce. We cannot afford everything we want. As individuals, incomes give us the ability to buy things produced using resources (land, labour, capital and enterprise), so we can think of incomes as a scarce resource.

A decision to go to university will involve a high commitment of both time and money; time that could have been spent earning money to boost personal resources or going out with friends. Of course, if someone gets a degree they are likely to earn more in the future – a benefit, so this must be weighed up against the cost of the time and money involved in gaining the qualification. For a teenager, the decision to spend £30 going out with friends might have to be weighed against buying a new top or pair of jeans.

Costs and benefits

Already in this chapter, we have come across a number of decisions involving **opportunity costs**. A teenager's decision to spend £30 going out with friends, perhaps to the cinema, or to buy a new top or pair of jeans would involve weighing up the **benefits** of enjoying a good night out against the **cost** of not being able to buy the new garment.

Benefits of going out:

■ enjoying a good night
■ enjoying the company of friends
■ avoiding offending friends by refusing to go out, and so on.

Costs of going out:

■ the enjoyment would only last for a single evening, whereas clothes would last for several months
■ a teenager might worry about reaction of friends if they felt their clothes were 'un-cool'
■ the 'feel-good' factor from wearing new clothes would be lost.

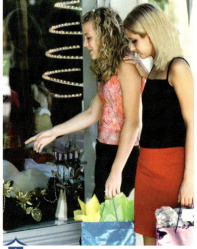
A *A choice between buying some clothes …*

B *… or going out with friends*

Objectives

Understand the basic economic problem.

Understand about choices and decisions.

Understand about costs and benefits when making decisions.

Understand about demand on resources and scarcity of resources.

Key terms

Scarcity: resources are limited compared with our 'needs' and 'wants'.

Choice: deciding between different options because our resources are limited.

Basic economic problem: resources are limited but 'needs' and 'wants' are infinite.

Resources: the land, labour, capital and enterprise used to produce goods and services.

Opportunity cost: something given up when we make a choice.

Benefits: the advantages of a particular choice.

Costs: the expenses and drawbacks of a particular choice.

Nathan has really set his heart on a new 'people-carrier' vehicle, but Tracy, who has a degree in computer-aided design, wants to design and build (with Nathan's reluctant help!) her dream kitchen. Each option will cost them around £20,000. The problem is that they cannot afford both.

Activity

1 Using two recent decisions you have made, list all the costs and benefits of your choice and explain, with reasons, how you came to your final decision.

Activities

2 List the costs and benefits to Nathan and Tracy of both the people-carrier and the new kitchen.

3 Justifying your choice, recommend to Nathan and Tracy whether they should buy the people-carrier or build the new kitchen.

■ How demand changes over the personal life cycle

Needs, wants and incomes change significantly over a lifetime. Initially, a person's **demand** is likely to be more for basic household goods. With a family, the demand will change to goods and services for the children. Once children have left home, people may start to take more meals out or more expensive holidays as demands on income will be lower. In retirement, incomes fall so people may need to cut back on expenditure. Tastes in products will also change, no doubt away from computer games! Depending on their savings, people may have to reduce their demand for non-essential goods and services.

Key terms

Demand: the quantity of a good or service that consumers are willing and able to purchase at a particular price.

AQA Examiner's tip

When answering questions on the needs of pensioners, do not assume that everyone over 65 lives in an old persons' care home.

1.3 Choosing to spend

■ Markets and how they work

Demand and the factors that affect spending

The demand is the quantity of all goods and services purchased at any given price. As the price increases for a good, the quantity demanded will fall, and vice versa. For example consumers will probably start using more gas as British Gas have dropped their prices by 10 per cent. There are many other **factors affecting demand** apart from price, however, that affect our spending decisions:

- income level – the most important
- advertising and branding influence desire and loyalty for a product
- prices of substitutes (similar goods) and complements (for example fuel is a complement of cars)
- fashion.

The part played by businesses – 'supply'

Businesses produce goods and services for people to buy so that the business can make a profit. The amount they offer for sale is called '**supply**'. Businesses tend to supply more, the higher the price. The price they charge has to cover the costs of the resources used in production. **Factors affecting supply** and how much businesses charge include:

- cost of raw materials
- wage rates – overtime may need to be paid for higher output
- productivity of the workers.

Activities

1. Explain why advertising on the internet might lead to more sales than advertising on TV.

2. Why might the demand for luxury products fall in a recession?

Markets and why market prices change

When buyers and sellers come together, a **market** is formed. For very expensive items, like a house, the buyer and seller negotiate a selling price individually. For most goods and services, however, the **market price** is determined by the amount buyers are willing to pay and the price that businesses need to be paid to cover their costs. If a good does not sell well, suppliers have to lower their price. Eventually, the price will settle at a point where supply equals demand, known as the market price.

Objectives

Understand how markets operate and how businesses compete.

Understand the reasons why prices change.

Understand the effects of competition between businesses on prices, products, quality.

Did you know ??????

For more than a year, food manufacturers have been gradually reducing package sizes and raising prices, claiming they had little choice because of large recent increases in the cost of raw ingredients like corn, soybeans and wheat.

Source: Adapted from an article in the New York Times, 27 November 2008

Key terms

Factors affecting demand: things that cause consumers to buy more or less of a product at a given price.

Supply: the quantity of a good or service that businesses will offer for sale at a particular price.

Factors affecting supply: things that cause suppliers to offer more or less of a good or service at a particular price.

Markets: a market exists whenever buyers and sellers come together.

Market price: the price that buyers and sellers agree on for a particular good or service.

Prices change when there are changes in demand or supply. For example, when oil prices are rising, costs for all companies rise, as oil is needed for energy, transport and heating. Businesses will have to raise their prices to cover increased production costs. A serious health scare can cause a big fall in demand, and prices will have to fall to maintain sales.

Activity

3 Find a product where the price has recently risen or fallen sharply. Research the reasons for this rise or fall.

Competition

Usually there is more than one supplier for each type of good, so businesses face **competition**. They have to fight to win consumers from other businesses by:

- advertising and branding (e.g. the Andrex puppy and toilet rolls)
- improving quality
- changing the design and features (e.g. frequent updates of mobile phones)
- lowering the price by improving production methods (e.g. by being more energy efficient).

Consumers can benefit greatly from competition through:

- lower prices (e.g. price wars – supermarkets compete to provide better value)
- greater variety (e.g. supermarkets stock value, branded and premium versions of the same good)
- better quality (e.g. McDonald's improved the quality of its coffee by buying better quality beans).

There can also be disadvantages:

- Quality can be lowered as businesses try to cut costs (e.g. some companies sell clothes and electrical goods that are cheaper now than they were 15 years ago, but do not last so long).
- After-sales service can suffer if too many resources are put into sales.

Did you know ??????

At the start of 2009, British Gas announced it would reduce gas prices by 10 per cent. This was expected to kick start a price war between energy distribution companies. Gas prices were generally expected to fall during the year because of increased competition and because world demand for energy was falling.

AQA Examiner's tip

To explain why the price of a product has changed, be sure to analyse fully what has happened to the costs of production.

Key terms

Competition: the process of trying to beat others (e.g. trying to gain more customers).

Activities

4 If the price of oil rises, explain what would happen to sales of

a cars

b products made out of plastic

c bananas.

5 Explain why competition among food manufacturers might make it difficult for manufacturers to reduce package sizes or increase prices.

1.4 Choosing to save

■ Why do people save?

By saving, people decide not to spend all of their income now, but to keep some of it to pay for things they might need in the future. They do this because of uncertainty about future events in their life cycle. They may need to delay spending now so that in the future they can pay for emergencies and planned purchases.

Some of the reasons to save might include:

- to buy something special, like a car, a wedding celebration or a house
- to put money aside for an emergency such as replacing a fridge or TV
- to save for retirement.

A *Some people save for a special occasion*

Case study

Finance was very tight when Nathan got his first job. He had a student loan and needed a mortgage to buy his first house. There was no opportunity to save. Luckily, Tracy had a small inheritance that she had saved for a 'rainy day'.

However, following all Nathan's promotions and having paid off some of the mortgage, they were in a position to start saving. The trouble was, Nathan found it difficult to save when there were so many tempting goods and services that he wanted to buy. Tracy had to keep reminding him that soon there would be university expenses to pay for their sons.

B *There were so many tempting things to buy*

Activities

1 Outline Nathan's and Tracy's attitudes to saving. What is the main difference between them?

2 Tracy was anxious to keep some money aside for a rainy day. Explain why she might think it necessary to save.

■ Methods of saving

If someone is in a position to save (i.e. their net income after tax is higher than their regular outgoings), they have a wide selection of places where they can deposit money. These include:

- high-street **banks** (such as NatWest and HSBC) and **building societies** (like West Bromwich or Derbyshire)
- internet-only banks (such as Smile, Cahoot)
- National Savings and Investments
- **Post Office card account** – a simple account mainly for pensioners or those receiving benefits. It only allows you to withdraw cash using the card. You cannot go overdrawn, but you won't get any charges.

C *There are many different methods of saving – how do you save?*

Key terms

Bank/building society savings account: an account for which the main objective is to gain interest and keep money safe.

Post Office card account: savings account offered by the Post Office.

There are also many different types of account within each of the main savings institutions:

- savings accounts and Individual Savings Accounts (ISAs) – savings on which interest payments are tax free
- fixed-term investment accounts – savings cannot be withdrawn for an agreed length of time (term)
- share-based savings (e.g. unit trusts) – these are savings products that spread risk by investing in a range of shares
- government securities – bonds issued by the government through National Savings and Investments.

The government also tries to encourage people to save, as saving is part of good financial management. Through ISA accounts, people can save a set amount of cash every tax year (£3,600 in 2009), and the interest earned on this saving is free of tax. For someone in work, the government also allows them to reclaim income tax relief on contributions made to a pension (for the tax year 2008–9, the annual allowance was £235,000). See **www.direct.gov.uk** for more details.

- Unfortunately, the government charges tax on interest from all other savings accounts. You will often see savings interest rates advertised as 'gross' or 'net'.
- Gross interest is the interest rate before tax has been deducted.
- Net interest is the rate you receive after tax has been taken off.

Identifying suitable forms of saving for different situations

D

Account	Reward	Risk	Short-, medium- or long-term	Ease of withdrawing money
Savings accounts	Low–medium	Low	Short–long	Easy – unless notice of withdrawal is required
ISA accounts	Low–medium	Low	Medium–long	Easy
National Savings and Investment account	Low	Very low	Medium–long	Often requires written notice of withdrawal
Unit trusts	Medium–high	Medium–high	Long	Obtaining your money may take some time

Comparison of the key features of different savings methods

The table **D** shows that the various savings methods have differing combinations of risk, reward and ease of withdrawing money. More information is given on interest rates and fixed-term savings in the next section.

Because of this, it is very important that people think about the reason they are saving the money before choosing the type of savings product.

E *Think about why you save before you choose a savings product*

Activity

3 Nathan, his family and friends need to put money aside for the purposes listed below. For each purpose, research and recommend a suitable savings product, explaining carefully your reasons.

- Noah, his son, wants to buy the latest computer game 'The Zombies are Hungry!'
- Tracy's friend, Husna, wants to buy a car.
- Both Nathan and Tracy want to put money aside for Noah's university education in eight years' time.
- Nathan knows that he must start putting money away for his retirement. He is currently 35.

Interest rates

The table at **D** on the previous page shows that the rate of interest obtained on savings partly depends on the length of time the money is tied up (the 'term'). Generally, if you can leave your money longer, you will get a higher rate of interest (a higher return) – though this is not always the case.

You can also obtain higher rates of interest if you save larger amounts or if you have to give notice, which means telling the bank in advance that you wish to withdraw your savings.

The table at **G** shows an internet comparison of savings accounts from December 2008. The lower running costs of internet-only accounts mean that these offer higher interest. However not everyone will want to use these online accounts, believing that they are less safe or secure than going to their local bank or building society. Some people also prefer the customer-focus they receive in these branches.

F *There are a variety of reasons why people save*

G

Provider	Type of account	AER	Notice	Interest paid	Minimum balance
AA	Internet saver	6.46%	Instant	Monthly	£1
Alliance and Leicester	Online tracker	4.75%	Instant	Annually	£1

Source: www.which-savings-account-4u.co.uk

Savings accounts

Table **H** shows that by saving regular amounts every month or saving money for a fixed term, you usually get a higher interest rate. In the latter case, you get a guaranteed interest rate for the length of the term. These are suitable for people who do not need access to their money for the length of the term.

H

Provider	Account	AER	Duration	Interest paid	Minimum balance
Halifax	International regular saver	8%	Fixed term for 1 year	On maturity	£100
ICICI bank	2-year HiSAVE fixed rate	5.42%	Fixed term for 2 years	On maturity	£1

Source: www.which-savings-account-4u.co.uk

Activities

I

Balance	AER	Gross p.a. (before tax is deducted)	Net p.a. (after tax is deducted)
£100,000+	0.55%	0.55%	0.44%
£50,000+	0.50%	0.50%	0.40%

Source: Halifax Instant Saver 1 December 2008

4 Explain the difference between 'gross' and 'net' interest.

5 Explain why instant access means lower interest.

Key terms

Annual Equivalent Rate (AER): a figure quoted in savings advertisements to help people compare one savings product with another.

■ The Annual Equivalent Rate (AER)

The savings accounts offered above all quote the **Annual Equivalent Rate (AER)** of interest.

An AER is given so that the interest rate on different savings accounts can be accurately compared. It shows what the interest rate would be if interest was paid and compounded once each year. For example, on some accounts interest is added each month (see the AA Internet Saver account in Table **G**). In this case you would get interest being earned on interest throughout the year. This is known as compounding (when interest is earned on interest already received). Because of compounding, the total amount of interest you receive in one year would be higher if credited monthly than if calculated only once, at the end of the year. The AER converts the monthly rate into a figure equivalent to the annual rate. The AER also removes the effect of any temporary promotional offers, that disappear within a few months, but which distort 'Best Buy' comparison tables.

Activities

J

Term – fixed ISA	AER	Gross p.a. (before tax is deducted)
1 Year £30,000+	5.50%	5.50%
1 Year £500+	5.00%	5.00%
2 Years £500+	4.00%	4.00%

Source: Fixed-rate Halifax ISA Saver – 1 December 2008

6 The net interest on the ISAs is not shown above. Why not?

7 Give possible explanations for why the two one-year fixed-term ISAs offer different rates of interest.

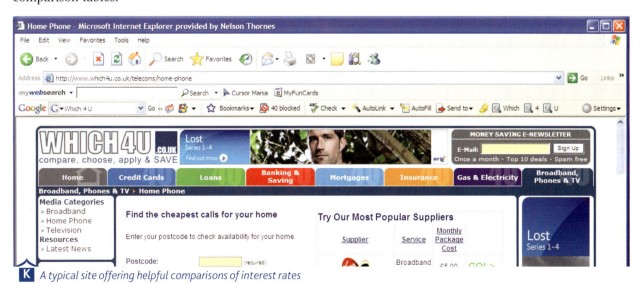

K *A typical site offering helpful comparisons of interest rates*

■ Risk and reward

For someone looking for potentially more return on their money or **reward,** they will usually have to consider a longer-term investment with more **risk**. Shares, unit trusts or government securities may be suitable. The higher reward wanted, the riskier the investment will be – in other words, they could also lose a lot of money!

Most people will seek to spread their risk by putting their money into different kinds of investment product, many of which are traded on the **stock market**.

Some of the riskier but potentially higher-return methods of saving are:

■ **Shares:** These represent a unit of ownership in a company. Most people buy several shares at a time, through a broker. A broker is someone who buys or sells on behalf of another. Often the broker is a bank (broker services are now commonly offered online as well).

If Marks and Spencers' shares are trading for £2.50 per share, and you wish to invest £1000, you buy 400 shares, plus pay a commission to the broker each time you buy or sell.

Shares are a risk. If the company is likely to make a large profit, demand for its shares will rise, causing the share price to rise. However, as happened with many companies in 2008, if the business is thought to be having trouble, investors sell their shares and the share price falls. In the UK, shares are bought and sold by traders on the London Stock Exchange (LSE). The most famous index produced by the LSE is the FTSE 100, which gives the average change in share prices for the largest 100 companies in the UK for that day.

Key terms

Reward: the return received for taking risks.

Risk: the chance that something may not succeed and its consequence.

Stock market: the place where stocks, shares and bonds are traded.

Shares: certificate representing a unit of ownership in a company.

L *Different kinds of investment product: a vending machine selling gold bars, installed in Frankfurt airport, summer 2009. The price is calculated according to real-time stock market rates*

Case study

Lloyds TSB share price

Below is a graph **M** showing how Lloyds TSB's share price changed over the period January – November 2008. As you can see, the price of their shares fell over the period from a high of around 500p, to a low of just over 150p in November. This was not good news for people who owned Lloyds TSB shares!

M *Share price*

Source: Lloyds TSB Group plc

N *Reijo - economist and entrepreneur*

Reijo explains what's happening to the share price:

'Looking at the graph on page 20 you can see Lloyds TSB's share price changing all the time. This is because the demand and supply of the share keeps changing. When more shareholders want to sell Lloyds TSB shares than buy them, the price falls (eg, May to July). The opposite is true when more people wish to buy than sell (eg, April and October).'

- **Unit trusts:** This is an investment fund where many investors, who probably know little about share buying, pool their money and buy a variety of shares. They do this to benefit from greater security, as the fund is managed by an experienced fund manager. It is, however, important to choose a fund with a good track record.

- Gilts (**government securities**): These are bonds (IOUs), known as bills of exchange, issued by the government. They pay a fixed rate of interest twice a year. Gilts are considered very safe investments as the government is unlikely to go bankrupt or to fail to pay back the interest payments. Gilts are bought and sold on the stock market by brokers or high-street banks. Although fairly safe, their price can go down as well as up, just like shares.

> **Key terms**
>
> **Unit trusts:** a pooled investment fund usually in shares-based investments.
>
> **Government securities:** stocks, bonds and bills of exchange issued by a government to raise the funds.

○ *The London Stock Exchange, EC4*

1.5 Choosing to borrow money

Why borrow?

People's spending needs change over their personal life cycle so it is often necessary to **borrow** money by means of a **loan** to make large purchases (e.g. to pay for an expensive holiday or buy a car) which can be repaid from earnings over an agreed period of time (the **term of a loan**). Sometimes emergencies crop up (e.g. the oven has to be replaced). If there are not enough savings, borrowing enables an essential item to be bought immediately.

Methods of borrowing

The most common forms of personal borrowing are:

- **Mortgage** – a loan to finance the purchase of real estate (e.g. a house). A mortgage is secured on the house, which remains the property of the bank until it is fully paid off.
- **Credit card** – cards that may be used repeatedly to buy products and services on **credit** or to borrow money up to a pre-arranged limit. Each month, you must pay at least the minimum repayment required (usually around 3–5 per cent) of the outstanding balance. You can pay more if you want, and this will reduce the interest you pay. Credit card interest rates are high.
- **Store card** – cards that may be used to buy products and services on credit from the shop that issued the card, up to a pre-arranged limit. Repayment terms are similar to credit cards.
- **Personal loan** – a loan given for personal or household use (e.g. to buy expensive household items like new furniture).
- **Hire purchase** – instalment plan whereby the loan company owns the item, but it becomes yours when the agreement (**debt**) is fully paid off.
- **Overdraft** – borrowing up to an agreed limit on a current account. Overdrafts must be paid back on demand.

A

Type of loan	Interest rate	Is security needed?	Flexibility of repayments
Mortgages	Low	Yes – your house is security	Very little – the amount changes when there are changes in the base rate
Credit and store cards	High	No	High – you can pay the minimum, or more if you wish
Personal loans	Medium	No	None
Hire purchase	Medium	Yes – the purchase acts as security	None
Overdraft	High	No	High – but make sure you do not go over the agreed limit

Choosing a suitable loan for your circumstances

Case study

Nathan's friend Malik has an expensive car and house, and spends a lot on new clothes. Nathan and Tracy suspect that he may be near the limit on his credit cards. Malik also has his own business and although his average monthly income has been £5,000 a month over the past two years, it is not guaranteed, especially with difficult business conditions in 2009. Malik will need to borrow money if he is to pay for:

- another new car that will cost £25,000
- flight tickets to Spain that will cost £230
- the purchase of a small flat near London that will cost £300,000.

Activity

1 For each of Malik's purchases, recommend, with reasons, a suitable method of borrowing.

Interest rates and APR

The interest rate is the cost of taking out a loan. The higher the rate of interest, the more you have to repay in total. For any given repayment time, the higher the interest rate, the higher the monthly repayments will be.

Annual Percentage Rate (APR) is the interest rate quoted on loan and credit card advertisements. It helps to compare the cost of different loans. It takes into account the basic interest rate and how it is charged (e.g. daily or annually), plus any additional costs (e.g. arrangement fees). All lenders must publish and calculate the APR in the same way. This makes it easier for borrowers to compare the cost of loans from different providers, and to compare the cost of different types of loan, eg a mortgage compared to a personal loan. Lenders generally charge a higher APR for riskier loans. If the APR is higher, the monthly repayments will be higher too.

Mortgages charge lower interest because the bank can sell the house and get its money back if someone defaults on the repayments, and the loan is usually over a much longer term. Credit cards are more expensive because no security has to be provided by the card holder.

A loan is usually repaid in monthly instalments – equal amounts every month for the period of the loan. At the beginning of the loan period there is a lot of money owed (the capital), so the interest payments are high. Each loan instalment is made up of two parts, an interest payment and a repayment of the amount borrowed (the capital). As you make more repayments you pay off more of the capital, so the interest component of each instalment reduces and the amount of capital paid off increases (see diagram **B**).

Activity

2 A building society is offering a mortgage at 5.5 per cent, plus an arrangement fee of £800. A bank is offering an interest rate of 6.0 per cent with a £200 fee. What do you need to know before deciding which mortgage to recommend?

AQA Examiner's tip

Be careful to link the type of borrowing to the particular borrowing needs in the question.

Key terms

Annual Percentage Rate (APR): the interest rate published on loans to help compare their true costs.

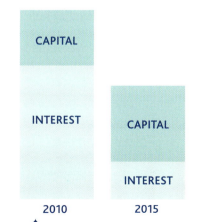

CAPITAL

INTEREST

CAPITAL

INTEREST

2010   2015

B *Repayment of capital compared with interest: the split of your payment changes over time*

1.6 Managing your money

The need for financial planning and budgeting

Financial planning and budgeting

Over the personal life cycle, we know that people's needs and wants will change greatly. Careful **financial planning** (budgeting) is needed to make sure that they will be able to meet these needs and wants. Individuals will get into debt problems if they consistently spend more than they earn. Budgeting can help to avoid this. A very simple **budget** looks like this:

Monthly net income	£1,500
Less:	
Monthly expenses (mortgage, food, etc.)	(£1,000)
Money available to spend or save	£500

As income or expenses change over the life cycle (e.g. when someone gets a job or a promotion), the figures can be adjusted. New spending and savings plans can be made to reflect changes in the life cycle. To stay clear of financial problems, budgeting is the key.

A **financial advisor** can help make more complicated plans that involve investments, and so on.

Some of these changes can be planned for. For example:

- buying (or not buying) expensive items, such as some designer clothes, a new phone, furniture, and so on
- university – fees and living expenses mean that a young person will need a student loan or money from parents
- buying or renting a house
- redundancy, sickness or disability
- retirement.

However, some changes happen unexpectedly. Unpredictable events mean that people need to save to have something in reserve. They may even have to take out a loan to cover an emergency. Planning for these uncertain events is one of the keys to avoiding financial problems.

Activities

Amanda's budget	
Monthly net income	£1200
Interest on savings	£50
Total monthly income	£1250
Less:	
Mortgage repayment	£300
Food	£200
Other	£500
Money available to spend or save	£ ?

1 Calculate the amount of money left over in Amanda's budget.

2 Interest rates have risen recently increasing the mortgage payments by 10 per cent. Calculate the effect on Amanda's budget.

3 Explain some other events that could change Amanda's budget. What action could she take to prevent these causing her financial problems?

What happens if you do not make effective financial plans?

Spending on credit cards is all too easy, and banks encourage people to do it. With more loans and growing credit card balances, it becomes ever more difficult to reduce what you owe. The interest charged will build up.

People who do get into serious debt problems, however, will probably need to use **debt management**. This involves seeing an expert who will help draw up a **debt management plan** to help sort out the situation. The plan will determine what an individual can afford to pay off each month. Very often the expert or debt counsellor can negotiate with some of the creditors (the people to whom money is owed, e.g. banks) to reduce the amount of interest paid over the period of the plan.

■ Ethical issues to do with saving

Banks use people's savings to finance their lending. They have a huge indirect impact on society through the organisations and individuals they finance and support with their loans. Deciding where to save can therefore cause a **social, moral or ethical dilemma**. Should we save with the bank that offers the highest interest on our savings, or one that has an **ethical lending policy**. Such a policy might be:

> 66 … to ensure that lending supports projects that are developed in a socially responsible manner, and reflect sound environmental management practices. 99

Source: www.equator-principles.com 5 May 2004.

Buying new shares in companies also supports their activities. Some businesses (e.g.Body Shop or the Cooperative Bank) have high ethical standards. These could include buying from businesses that pay their workers a fair wage or do not employ child labour, especially that from poorer countries, or have high environmental standards. Some businesses, such as armament producers, might be considered unethical and you may not wish to buy their shares.

Activities

4   List some business activities that you consider to be unethical.

5   Either individually or in small groups, try to find one or more banks that have a strong ethical lending policy.

6   Search websites for companies with high ethical standards and in which Nathan and Tracy would be happy to buy shares. Summarise some of their ethical standards.

■ Ethical issues to do with borrowing

There are also many ethical issues surrounding borrowing. Should people borrow if they might not be able to repay the money? From whom should they borrow? Those with good credit histories and secure incomes can get loans from reputable banks, which operate within the law. However, people refused credit from banks are often tempted to approach lenders operating illegally ('loan sharks') who make unsecured loans at very high interest rates, but charge astronomical interest, sometimes between 100 and 1000 per cent per year, using threats of violence if people fail to repay on time.

Key terms

Debt management: taking the help of an expert to solve a debt problem.

Debt management plan: a structured repayment plan.

Social, moral or ethical dilemma: a problem with no absolute right or wrong solution.

Ethical lending policy: a statement that loans will only be made to businesses that act in a socially responsible manner.

Ethics: the 'rights' and 'wrongs' of an issue.

Case study

Tracy and Nathan thought about the recommendations you made previously, and discussed what saving methods they were going to use. They were both clear on the fact that they wanted to save with an ethical bank. They were determined not to save with any banks that lend to oppressive political regimes, or to buy shares in unethical businesses.

Case study

Anna is unemployed. Her young daughter's birthday is coming up and Anna wants to buy her nice things like her friends have. No bank will lend her money so she has decided to borrow from a 'loan shark'.

Nathan and Tracy are still arguing over the people-carrier or the new kitchen.

Malik took out another loan to buy the new car he wanted. The recession means that he cannot be sure of his income for a year or so.

Activities

7   Is Anna right to borrow from a 'loan shark'?

8   Should Malik borrow to buy his car when he knows he might not be able to pay it back?

1

By now you should have a clear understanding of:

✔ how spending, saving and borrowing needs change at key points in the personal life cycle

✔ how the demand for goods and services changes throughout the personal life cycle

✔ how prices change due to the decisions of buyers and competing businesses in the market

✔ why people save and that potential rewards from savings reflect the degree of risk

✔ different methods of borrowing and how interest rates charged reflect the type of loan

✔ why financial planning is important.

Revision quiz

1 Choose the right answer. Spending over your limit on your credit card is a reason to:

a start saving money?

b borrow some more money to tide you over?

c start learning to manage your money better?

2 Choose the right answer. Everyone needs to use financial planning because:

a incomes are a scarce resource?

b needs and wants change over our personal life cycle?

c there is an opportunity cost to every decision we take?

3 List three main stages in the personal life cycle.

4 Explain how a person's income is likely to change at key points in their life cycle.

5 Give a definition of the basic economic problem.

6 List the four main categories of economic resource, giving an example of each.

7 List two costs and two benefits of taking a university degree.

8 Explain how an adult might go about making the decision to accept a new job.

9 List three things that might cause a change in the price of a pair of jeans.

10 Explain how the level of wages a business pays its employees might influence the prices it charges its customers.

11 Analyse the actions that a soft drinks business might take to compete against its rivals.

12 Explain two disadvantages a consumer might face because of increased competition between businesses.

13 Analyse the reasons for which a middle-aged couple might want to save.

14 State two methods suitable for long-term saving.

15 Analyse the issues that an ethical lender might consider when deciding to lend to a young couple.

16 Explain how interest rates could influence the amount a person: a saves b borrows.

17 Outline the typical relationship between risk and reward for savings products.

18 State a suitable method of borrowing to: a buy a house b pay for some new clothes.

19 Name one loan for which security is needed. Why does the bank ask for security?

20 Which types of people are typically given government social security benefits?

21 Explain what is meant by a budget and for what purpose it is used.

22 Explain how a debt management plan can help you get out of serious financial trouble.

2 Work

Aims

✔ Understand why people choose to work.

✔ Understand how specialisation and interdependence occurs in the workplace.

✔ Understand how the nature of work is changing – especially with the advance of ICT in the workplace.

✔ Understand the various ways in which people are paid.

✔ Understand the difference between gross and net pay – the deductions that are taken from gross pay.

✔ Understand how the supply of labour is affected by the decision on whether to work or not.

✔ Understand how the demand for labour is derived from the need for workers.

✔ Understand why wages differ between people and occupations.

✔ Understand the influence of the government on pay and working conditions.

✔ Understand the costs of unemployment to the individual.

✔ Understand how the government deals with unemployment of varying duration.

In this chapter we consider why people choose to work and how specialisation occurs in the workplace. We will look at how the nature of work is changing and also consider the reward for working and the different ways in which people are paid, along with the various deductions made from pay.

We look at the factors that determine whether or not someone will be willing to supply their labour. This is considered alongside the factors that determine how much labour a business will want to employ. Both the supply of and the demand for labour are brought together to show how wages are determined. Why wages differ between people and occupations is also examined.

Finally, we look at why someone may be unemployed along with the costs of unemployment and how the government aims to tackle unemployment.

2.1   Why people work and the nature of work

Work refers to *paid work* – where people perform jobs in exchange for money and other benefits. The person working is often referred to as an employee, while the business employing the worker(s) is known as the employer. This distinction is not clear when a person is self-employed (i.e. they work for themselves).

Why people work

There are a number of reasons why someone will choose to work. These can include pay and job satisfaction.

Pay

Many people will work **full-time** and the money received for this work will allow them to purchase goods (such as cars and clothes) and services, as well as pay for any other family members who do not work. Pay can be a **motivation** factor, so some people may work in order to provide money for a specific purpose. For example, many people who are students will also work **part-time**, or take **temporary** or **seasonal** work to supplement student grants or loans they receive.

Job satisfaction

Some people choose to work even when they do not obviously need the income. This could be because of:

- the social aspect of the job (e.g. the after-work sporting activities with colleagues)
- the enjoyment of a job (e.g. the job satisfaction achieved by being successful at work).

Objectives

Understand what is meant by work.

Understand the reasons people choose to work or not to work.

Understand what is meant by specialisation and interdependence and the benefits and drawbacks of specialisation.

Understand how the nature of work has changed through ICT and home working.

Key terms

Full-time: a worker who works the maximum number of hours required in the normal working week for a particular job.

Motivation: the reason that somebody does something.

Part-time: this refers to a worker who only works a fraction of the working week of a full-time employee.

Temporary employment: work that will only last for a specific period of time (usually a number of weeks or months).

Seasonal employment: work that is only required during a particular period of a year (e.g. some agricultural work).

Case study

Why people work

Here we have three different people who work for very different reasons.

Ali is 17 and works in his father's Indian restaurant. He is working part-time for eight hours a week. The money he earns is used to run his second-hand car. He doesn't expect to work in his current job for long as he is going to university next year.

Helen is 35. She works full-time as a nurse. She and her partner have two young children and a mortgage to pay. As a result, both she and her partner work full-time.

Harold has recently taken early retirement. He is 63 but misses the social environment of work. He has taken a job working in the local DIY chain. The money doesn't motivate Harold and he doesn't want to work more than a few hours per week.

Activities

1. Why does Ali choose to work only eight hours per week?

2. Why do both Helen and her partner choose to work full-time?

3. Give two reasons why Harold is not motivated by the money he receives from working.

Why people may not work

A large proportion of the UK adult population currently do not work. Some of the major reasons for this are described in the following sections.

> ### AQA Examiner's tip
>
> Don't confuse the motivation for working in the first place with what motivates someone who is currently working – they could well be different. Money is more of a motivator to get someone into work, while other factors (such as promotion opportunities) become more important once someone has a job.

The personal life cycle

In education	Bringing up children	Retired

A *Students may choose to remain in education rather than work*

B *Either parent may stay at home to raise children*

C *Workers can retire at 60 or 65 (or earlier if they have a sufficient pension)*

Education

An increasing number of people now remain in full-time education (usually university) until well into their early 20s. The number of older people choosing to attend university is also increasing.

> ### Activity
>
> **4** Assess the case for raising the school leaving age to 18. Try to include the viewpoints of different groups (e.g. business views).

Child care

People – usually women, but increasingly men – may choose not to work so that they can raise children. This is more likely to be the case if the parent is a lone parent or if the child carer's partner earns enough from his or her own job to provide for the whole family.

> ### Did you know ??????
>
> By 2013, young people in the UK will be expected to stay in school, training or workplace training until they are 18 years old.

> ### Did you know ??????
>
> The number of 'househusbands' (men who quit work to stay at home and look after children) rose between 1993 and 2007 by 83 per cent.
>
> Source: *Daily Mail*, 10 July 2007

Retirement

People may not work because they have officially retired. Although the official retirement age in the UK is 65 (for most people) many will retire early. However, this practice is decreasing as people live longer and also find that the state retirement pension is insufficient to fund their lifestyle.

Activity

5 Describe the different reasons why people may choose not to work during various stages of their lives.

Growth in services

As modern economies develop, there is a gradual shift in employment patterns. Employment in manufacturing and other secondary industries declines, and employment in the service sector grows. In the UK, many of the manufactured goods previously produced here are now imported, meaning that there is less need for manufacturing jobs.

Case study

Patterns of UK employment

The following table shows the numbers employed in selected industrial sectors of the UK economy.

D

Year	Manufacturing sector	Financial services sector	Total service sector
1988	5,283,000	3,983,000	19,504,000
1998	4,554,000	5,152,000	21,675,000
2008	3,138,000	6,668,000	25,574,000

Source: Office for National Statistics www.statistics.gov.uk

Activity

6 Describe the trends in UK employment by industrial sector over the last 20 years.

Specialisation

Specialisation (also known as the division of labour) refers to workers only employed on a small aspect of the work conducted in their workplace. Such a worker will not be involved fully in the production of the goods but will concentrate on a particular area of the production. As a result, workers become interdependent – they depend on each other for completing their own part of the production process.

Benefits of specialisation

- Workers can become more skilled if they focus on one task rather than be involved with the whole production process.
- Output can be produced more quickly as workers become more familiar with the reduced number of tasks that they are required to complete.

Key terms

Specialisation: where each worker concentrates on only one small aspect of the entire production process.

- Businesses can produce output at lower cost due to faster and more skilled workers and this saving may be shared with workers in higher wages.
- Workers can concentrate on the tasks that they are most skilled at.

Limitations of specialisation

- Workers and production will become interdependent. Workers will depend on each other in order to complete the overall output, which may cause problems if one area of production fails, through mistakes being made.
- Jobs will become boring if workers are only involved in a repeated, small part of the production process.
- Morale in the workplace may fall as jobs become more repetitive and absenteeism and labour turnover may rise.
- If a worker is absent, it may be hard to arrange cover for their section if workers are untrained in jobs other than their own.
- Workers will become less flexible and it will be harder to adapt if new types of goods need to be produced.

Information Communication Technology (ICT) and work

Advances in technology, especially in **ICT**, have had some effect on those in work. A number of features of ICT have changed how people work, and some are listed below.

The internet

The internet has changed how many businesses operate. The growth in online retailing removes the need for as many people to be employed in shops and other business outlets. However, some will have found new jobs in web-based businesses.

E-mail

E-mail has changed how we communicate at work – speeding up and easing how we can communicate with large numbers of people in our own companies and across the world. This reduces the need for telephone calls or letters.

Home working

The ability to use e-mail and the internet, as well as being able to access work-based computer networks from home, has led to an increase in the number of people who now work from home. Many people welcome **flexible working** as it helps them to manage both work and looking after a young family. This can help businesses to reduce costs as they may not have to provide as many facilities at their main offices as they would if all workers were based 'on site'.

E *Computers and e-mail have displaced typists and other workers – but created other jobs*

The reward for work

How people are paid

People are paid for the labour they supply. Generally, people are paid more the longer they work. However, there are a number of different ways that people are paid for their labour.

Salary

Salaries are stated as yearly earnings but are paid monthly. Although salaries are normally paid to those in full-time permanent jobs, it is possible for part-time workers to be paid a salary. Jobs paying salaries are more likely to be skilled, non-manual occupations.

Wage

Wages are calculated as an hourly rate multiplied by the number of hours worked. Wages are normally paid weekly. They are more likely to be paid for lower-skilled jobs, and for part-time or temporary work.

Commission

Workers paid by **commission** receive payments for achieving certain targets – often connected with sales. A worker who adds to the firm's sales receives a percentage of the sales value as reward. Commission encourages workers to achieve more sales. Workers can be paid partly or fully on commission.

Overtime payment

Businesses sometimes need workers to work longer hours. This is especially true when production needs to be higher than usual but that this will be temporary. Rather than employ more workers, a business will encourage its workforce to work longer hours. These extra hours are paid at a higher rate and are known as **overtime payments**.

Shift work payment

Some workers will not work traditional hours but will work in **shifts**. This often occurs when a business needs to be kept open for longer than the normal working day.

BACS

BACS stands for the Bankers' Automated Clearing Services and is a system used within the UK for allowing the electronic transfer of money between banks. This means that it avoids the need for paper-based documents when making payments. The payments can take up to three days to move from one bank account to another.

Key terms

Salary: pay stated as a yearly total.

Wage: pay calculated on an hourly rate, multiplied by the hours worked.

Commission: payment made to workers for achieving a certain target (e.g. sales levels).

Overtime payment: higher rate of pay for work in excess of normal working hours.

Shift work: work patterns that do not follow standard working hours.

Bankers' Automated Clearing Service (BACS): automatic transfer of funds between bank accounts (e.g. employer's to employee's).

Fringe benefits

These are when workers are paid in ways other than money. For example, fringe benefits of a job might include a company car, private health care or schooling fees. Fringe benefits are often paid for highly skilled, highly paid jobs.

1   Explain why businesses pay overtime rates rather than employ more workers on the lower standard wage rate.

Millward Ltd – pay structure

Mark Armstrong is the managing director of Millward Ltd – a firm manufacturing storage boxes for industry. It sells the boxes in both the UK and Europe. Armstrong is paid a salary of £60,000 per year and the directors are paid £45,000 per year. Other employees of Millward Ltd are paid as follows:

Production workers are paid wages of £6.50 per hour. They work a standard working week of 40 hours.

However, they often work extra hours in peak sales periods. The overtime rate is £9.00 per hour.

Sales staff are paid a basic salary of £15,000 and are also paid on commission – they receive a percentage of sales that they make. On average, the commission brings annual pay for sales staff up to £24,000 per year. Sales staff also receive fringe benefits (such as company cars) and they are paid for **expenses** (such as accommodation when they need to stay away from home).

A   *Production workers are paid differently to sales staff*

Activities

Answer these questions about Millward Ltd:

2   Why do the directors receive a salary rather than a wage?

3   How much would a production worker be paid in a week if they worked a full week plus seven hours overtime?

4   Why do you think that sales staff are paid partly on commission?

5   How do sales staff benefit from company cars?

Case study

Key terms

Expenses: payments given to workers to compensate for any expenditure necessary to complete their work.

B   *A company car: a desirable fringe benefit*

Wages and salaries

The payment for work will appear on a piece of documentation known as a pay slip. The pay slip will show the payment made to the worker and the various subtractions from this pay. These deductions will include the items listed in the next section.

Gross and net pay

Gross pay refers to the total amount of pay that a job will pay. However, the worker will not be able to keep the full amount of gross pay.

Deductions will be made (even if these are calculated at a later date in the case of self-assessment), which will reduce the amount that the worker actually receives.

Net pay refers to the pay after all deductions for tax, national insurance and pension contributions have been made. This is sometimes known as 'take-home pay' as it is the final amount.

Gross pay is useful to know as it allows comparisons between different jobs. Net pay is not strictly comparable as the amount of deductions will depend on various factors, such as the level of income and the type of pension.

Deductions on a pay slip

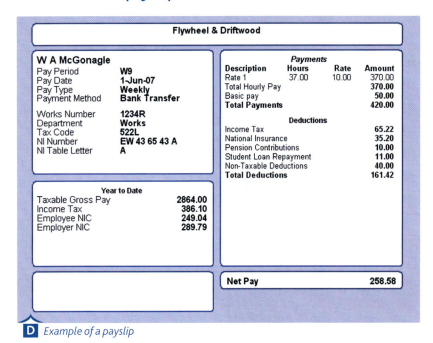

Flywheel & Driftwood

W A McGonagle
Pay Period — W9
Pay Date — 1–Jun–07
Pay Type — Weekly
Payment Method — Bank Transfer

Works Number — 1234R
Department — Works
Tax Code — 522L
NI Number — EW 43 65 43 A
NI Table Letter — A

Payments			
Description	Hours	Rate	Amount
Rate 1	37.00	10.00	370.00
Total Hourly Pay			370.00
Basic pay			50.00
Total Payments			**420.00**

Deductions	
Income Tax	65.22
National Insurance	35.20
Pension Contributions	10.00
Student Loan Repayment	11.00
Non-Taxable Deductions	40.00
Total Deductions	**161.42**

Year to Date	
Taxable Gross Pay	2864.00
Income Tax	386.10
Employee NIC	249.04
Employer NIC	289.79

Net Pay	258.58

D *Example of a payslip*

Income tax

Income tax is a tax on money paid to the worker. Although not all income is taxed, the income tax will be paid as a percentage of earnings.

People only pay income tax on earnings above a tax-free allowance. The percentage rate paid in income tax depends on the level of income,

C *Payslips: they give ... and they take away*

which is indicated by a **tax code**. As incomes rise, the percentage rate of income tax paid will rise.

Income tax in the UK is paid in two main ways:

- Pay as you earn (PAYE), where tax is deducted by the employer before income is paid to the worker.
- Self-assessment (SA) for workers who are self-employed – tax is paid by the worker.

National insurance

National insurance contributions (NIC) are paid by employees on incomes to build up an entitlement to certain benefits and the state pension. Like income tax, national insurance is paid as a percentage of income earned. The rates at which is it paid are different to those of income tax.

Pension contributions

Some workers will pay fewer NICs because they make payments to either a private or a company pension scheme. Workers pay a percentage of their income, which will then be invested. The worker will receive the pension when reaching retirement age (65 for most UK workers).

Other deductions

There may be other deductions from a worker's income, such as:

- trade union subscriptions
- staff association membership fees
- student loan repayments.

In addition, if you're an employee, your employer must give you certain documents – forms **P45** and **P60** – about the tax you pay. These are not given out monthly but only at the end of the tax year, and when you leave the company.

> **Key terms**
>
> **Tax code:** workers have different tax codes which relate to the different amount of tax-free allowance each worker has.
>
> **National insurance contribution (NIC):** a tax paid by workers which entitles the payee to qualify for benefits when and if necessary.
>
> **Pension contributions:** a deduction from a worker's pay that is meant to contribute to a future retirement pension.
>
> **P45:** a document provided by an employer when a worker leaves the organisation.
>
> **P60:** a document provided by an employer on a yearly basis showing total pay and deductions for the year.

> **Activities**
>
> 6   State four items that might be deducted from a worker's gross pay.
>
> 7   Referring to Figure **D**, what percentage of gross pay has been deducted from W. A. McGonagle's wages?

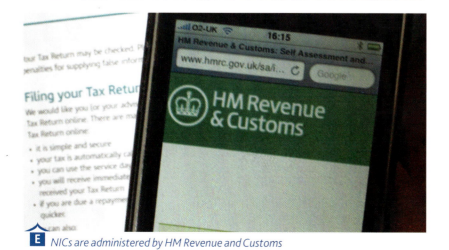

E *NICs are administered by HM Revenue and Customs*

Supply of labour

The supply of labour refers to the amount of work each worker is willing to perform. Each worker has a decision about whether or not to work. In effect, each worker can decide how to split their time between work and leisure.

The supply of labour is affected by a combination of monetary and non-monetary factors.

Monetary factors

The main factor that determines the supply of labour is the level of wages offered. The higher the wage rate or salary, the more willing a worker will be to supply their labour. This is because each hour worked becomes more valuable to the worker and as a result it becomes more tempting to work more.

Non-monetary factors

In addition to the wage rate, there are various non-monetary factors that influence how much a worker wants to work.

Gender

Traditionally, women were less willing to enter the labour force and supply their labour. However, this trend has changed. Although there is still a slightly higher proportion of men in the labour force, the proportion of women working has grown. This is due to:

- changing cultural attitudes – it is now more acceptable for women to work
- a decline in primary and secondary sector industries, more likely to recruit men rather than women
- changes in legislation making it easier for women to work while raising a family
- changes in the tax and benefit system, rewarding those with children who return to the workforce.

Ethnic origin

Traditionally, workers of non-white origin were less likely to be employed. Over the last two decades this has changed (especially for males) and those classified as 'White British' are more likely to be unemployed than other ethnic origin groups. However, this is a controversial issue and the reasons for this are not clear.

Taxation

Income tax reduces how much of a wage or salary a worker is allowed to keep. If income tax is reduced, then workers keep more of their pay, thereby creating a greater incentive to work than before. The overall supply of labour (people wanting to work) will increase.

Activity

Ethnic origin and educational qualifications

Look at this chart on race and GCSE attainment.

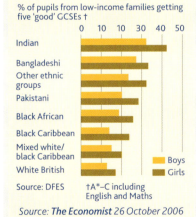

% of pupils from low-income families getting five 'good' GCSEs †

Source: DFES   †A*–C including English and Maths

Source: *The Economist* 26 October 2006

A *Educational achievement among low-income families by ethnic origin*

1. What patterns of employment may you expect to find based on the table? Explain your answer.

State benefits

Benefits are provided in the UK for those looking for work but not currently working. If benefit payments are sufficiently low, workers will be more willing to supply their labour as they cannot afford to remain out of work as long as they could if benefit payments were higher.

B

UK weekly benefit payments to those not in work for 2008	
Income support (aged 18–24)	£47.95
Income support (25 and over)	£60.50
Couple (both aged 25 and over)	£94.95

Source: Department for Work and Pensions

Activity

2   Some have argued that reducing benefits would increase the supply of labour. Using this data, decide whether you think that this is the case and why.

Demand for labour

The demand for labour comes from businesses that need workers to produce their goods and services. However, the demand for labour is unlike the demand for most goods and services.

Derived demand

Businesses don't demand workers for their own sake but because businesses need workers to produce goods and services for the firm to sell. This is known as a derived demand. The demand for labour (i.e. for workers) is a derived demand.

Government influence and the demand for labour

The UK government will indirectly affect the demand for labour. This is because it will influence through legislation how much a business must spend on a worker in addition to the wage that it pays. Some of these influences are as follows:

- right to paid holiday (to be increased to 5.6 times the normal working week in 2009)
- maternity/paternity pay (new mothers can receive a proportion of their existing pay for up to 39 weeks of maternity leave, and fathers can take up to two weeks' fully paid leave from work).

How wages are determined

The market wage refers to the wage rate that would be paid if the demand for labour and the supply of labour were to match exactly. The market wage would ensure those wanting to work could find work at this wage rate, and that businesses could find workers to employ.

If the wage rate was not set at this market rate, the following would occur:

- If the wage was higher, then more people would want to supply their labour than there were jobs available.
- If the wage rate was lower, then businesses would want to recruit more people than were willing to supply their labour.

Differences in wages

The wage rate for a particular job is determined by the demand for and the supply of labour. However, there is not one wage rate for all workers. Workers are paid different amounts depending on their job. These differences are known as wage differentials. There are a number of reasons that explain these, as follows.

Activities

3   Assess the case for new health and safety legislation to increase worker protection in the UK. (Hint – what impact would this have from a business's viewpoint?)

4   How much is maternity pay currently in the UK?

Reasons for differences in wages

Training and skills

Jobs that require more training and higher skills are likely to be paid more. This is because there are fewer people with these skills or level of training and businesses will need to pay more to ensure that they can attract these workers.

C

UK average weekly pay by occupational background for 2008

All employees	£471.90	Managers and senior officials	£812.40
Professional occupations	£694.90	Associate professional and technical occupations	£532.50
Administrative and secretarial occupations	£327.00	Skilled trade occupations	£458.50
Personal service occupations	£250.00	Sales and customer service occupations	£203.50
Process, plant and machine operatives	£421.60	Elementary occupations	£238.60

Source: www.statistics.gov.uk

Activities

5 Based on the weekly pay data, which two occupational groups have the highest weekly pay?

6 Analyse why skilled trade occupations pay more than sales and customer service occupations.

7 Apart from training, why might managers receive higher pay than professional workers?

Gender

Women are likely to be paid less than men. This is partly due to women being more likely to take a career break to raise children meaning that they miss out on training and promotion opportunities. Thirty years ago, women earned approximately two-thirds of men's earnings. However, this differential has narrowed so that women's wages are now around 85 per cent of men's.

Age

Older workers are likely to be paid more than younger workers. This is because they are likely to have more experience and possess the skills needed for the higher-paid jobs.

AQA Examiner's tip

Although older workers are usually paid more than younger workers, this is more about the experience the worker has rather than the age itself.

UK pay by age and gender

This chart shows the median weekly income for different age groups and also for males and females.

£ per week

Men

Women

D *Median weekly pay by gender*
Source: National Statistics Online www.statistics.gov.uk

Activities

8 Why do you think a gap exists at all between male and female earnings?

9 Explain what government policies could narrow this gap.

Trade unions

Trade unions are organisations that workers can decide to join. They protect workers and negotiate for higher wages for their members. They can achieve this by the threat of industrial action. Trade unions can call members out on strikes (where they refuse to work for a period of time) in order to encourage businesses to pay higher wages.

Government influence

In the 1990s, the UK government introduced a **minimum wage**. Before this some employers paid unfairly low wages. The minimum wage is the legal minimum hourly rate that can be paid to workers. It varies depending on the age of the worker.

Case study

Regional pay differences

The following shows the mean annual pay for full-time workers in the UK for 2008 across the regions of the UK.

E

London	£40,354	South	£27,003
UK	£26,020	East	£24,765
Scotland	£23,728	North West	£23,499
East Midlands	£23,287	South West	£23,135
West Midlands	£22,944	Yorkshire & Humber	£22,881
Northern Ireland	£21,465	Wales	£21,380
North East	£21,290		

Source: Office for National Statistics www.statistics.gov.uk

Why do wage rates change?

Surpluses of labour

If there is a surplus of labour, then more people want to work in a particular occupation than the number of jobs available. This is likely to lead to lower wages in this occupation as businesses can afford to pay less as there are more workers available.

Shortages of labour

If there is a shortage of labour in a particular industry, businesses will need to offer higher wages. This will encourage more workers to supply their labour for that industry.

Case study

UK labour shortages

Here is a list of some of the current occupations where there is a shortage of labour.

Project managers for property development and construction
Civil engineers   Chemical engineers   Veterinary surgeons
Secondary education teachers of maths and science   Geologists
Quantity surveyors   Skilled ballet dancers   Ship and hovercraft officers
Skilled chefs   Skilled senior care workers   Skilled sheep shearers

Source: www.ukba.homeoffice.gov.uk/

Activities

10 Why do you think the minimum wage was introduced in the UK?

11 What effect will this have on the demand for labour and supply of labour?

12 Was the introduction of the minimum wage justified?

13 In the UK, trade union powers have been reduced over the last 20 years. What effect will this have had on the demand for labour?

14 Using the idea of supply and demand, explain why footballers are paid more than rugby players.

Activity

15 Based on this data, which region had the highest and lowest pay for 2008? Explain why the level of pay is different in these two regions.

Key terms

Minimum wage: lowest legal hourly rate that can be paid.

Activity

16 Based on the shortages of labour, what do you think will happen to the pay for these positions? Explain your reasoning.

If the government was keen to ensure that these positions were filled, what action could it take?

Unemployment refers to those who are not currently working but are seeking work. We have already seen reasons why someone may choose not to work. We will now consider the case of people who want to work but cannot find employment and why this is a problem.

▮ Costs of unemployment to the individual

Unemployment creates costs for society and the economy as a whole. The costs of unemployment for the individual are as follows:

Monetary costs of unemployment

A person who is unemployed will not receive any income, except for benefit payments. As stated earlier in this chapter, the benefits paid to the unemployed are dependent on personal circumstances (e.g. single/married/with children), but the amount is significantly below the average weekly pay in the UK of almost £500.

A *Jobcentreplus aims to match vacancies …*

B *… to unemployed individuals*

Non-monetary costs of unemployment

Loss of skills

The longer someone remains unemployed, the more skills they lose. They will not be up to date with the latest on-the-job training.

Health

Those who are unemployed are more likely to suffer from poor health. This is especially true when it comes to mental health issues.

Family breakdown

The unemployed are more likely to experience family problems, with higher marital breakdown rates.

UK regional unemployment (April 2007–March 2008)

C

Region	%	Region	%
North East	6.4%	North West	5.7%
Yorkshire and the Humber	5.2%	East Midlands	5.2%
West Midlands	6.3%	East	4.2%
London	6.7%	South East	4.1%
South West	3.8%	Wales	5.6%
Scotland	4.6%	Northern Ireland	4.0%

Source: www.statistics.gov.uk

Activities

1 How could the government use this data for encouraging the unemployed to relocate?

2 Outline how the government could encourage the unemployed to relocate to other regions in order to fill job vacancies.

Duration of unemployment

Many of the costs of unemployment to the individual are made worse by an extended period of unemployment. For short periods of unemployment, the costs are less severe.

UK long-term unemployment

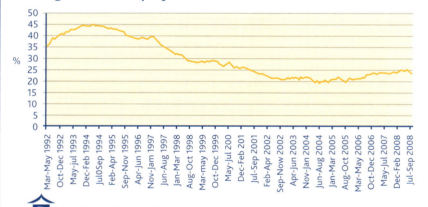

D *Duration of unemployment*

Source: National Statistics Online www.statistics.gov.uk

The chart shows the proportion of unemployment that is made up of long-term unemployment (i.e. unemployed for at least one year).

Activities

3 Describe the trend in UK long-term unemployment.

4 Is this trend a problem for the UK?

E *Older people may find it harder to get jobs*

Why does the duration of unemployment vary?

The reasons for the various durations of unemployment will include:

Skills and training

The more highly skilled a person is, the more likely they are to find new jobs when they are unemployed.

Qualifications

School leavers without formal qualifications may face longer periods of unemployment because they are considered to be less attractive to businesses.

Age

Older people may find it harder to get jobs because they often expect higher wages, and they are also considered to be 'too old' to train for new positions. However, age-related discrimination is illegal.

Did you know ??????

Laws banning age discrimination in the workplace were only introduced in 2006 in the UK.

Activity

5 Explain what sort of skills a person will lose if they remain unemployed for a long period of time.

Government strategies to help the unemployed

The government is rightly concerned about unemployment and has launched a number of policies to tackle both the level of unemployment, and also policies to deal with the duration of unemployment. These policies have been specifically designed for the different types of people who are unemployed. This is connected with the personal life cycle.

Tax allowances

Tax allowances allow people to earn up to a certain level before they start paying income tax. This is partly designed to ensure that the unemployed who take on jobs will not be financially worse off once they lose any unemployment-related benefits.

Jobseekers' allowance

The benefit payments to the unemployed are now linked to the person providing evidence that they are actively seeking work. This reduces the problem of the unemployed remaining on benefits indefinitely.

Working tax credits

Older unemployed people are likely to have family commitments. Taking a job may mean that they not only lose unemployment benefit, but they might have high costs of child care once they are working. As a result, the government lets those who have taken jobs receive benefits through working tax credits. This means that they don't lose all the benefits that they received while unemployed.

New deal

This policy focuses on providing training for people who have been unemployed for an extended duration. It particularly concentrates on those aged under 25 because it is believed that they are most likely to be unemployed due to lack of skills.

⬭links

www.jobcentreplus.gov.uk

F *The high costs of childcare can be claimed back through the tax credits system*

G *The government's New Deal*

Education

The government is encouraging more students to undertake vocation qualifications in schools and colleges. The introduction of a range of vocational diplomas is intended to ensure that those students who find academic study difficult do not leave education unprepared for the world of work.

All students have been affected by changes in government education policy. The introduction of key and functional skills (such as ICT and communication skills) is meant to equip students with skills which are increasingly important for employment.

Apprenticeships

Apprentices work alongside experienced staff and gain job-specific skills. The apprentice will normally receive training with a local training provider such as a college possibly on a day-release scheme (i.e. one day per week away from the workplace). This helps both the business (as apprentices don't get the full wage as a normal employee) but also helps the apprentice as they will gain skills that make them employable.

⦿links

www.apprenticeships.org.uk/

H *Young people on apprenticeships*

The unemployed and government policy

Lizzie Maclean was made unemployed when her office relocated overseas. She is 32 years old and has many years' experience in clerical work and the appropriate qualifications for work of a similar nature.

Jimmy Lam has never had a full-time permanent job. He is now 22 years old and has been receiving income support for three years. Jimmy is now undertaking training in ICT to make him more employable. However, he is not particularly interested in more training.

Carwyn Bell is 43 and is married with three children. He is a fork lift truck driver and was recently made unemployed. He can find work but for lower pay.

Case study

Activities

6 Which of the people mentioned in the case study would the government be most concerned about getting back to work?

7 Why do you think this is the case?

8 Explain why the government might be concerned about rising levels of unemployment.

2

By now you should have a clear understanding of:

✔ why people choose to work

✔ why people choose not to work

✔ how specialisation occurs within the workplace

✔ the benefits and drawbacks of specialisation

✔ how ICT has affected how we work

✔ the different ways in which people are paid

✔ the deductions that are subtracted from a worker's income

✔ what factors affect the supply of labour

✔ what factors affect the demand for labour

✔ why wages differ according to person and occupation

✔ how wages rates are affected by changes in the demand for and supply of labour

✔ what the costs of unemployment are to the individual

✔ why the duration of unemployment varies

✔ what strategies the government uses to deal with unemployment.

Revision quiz

1 Give three explanations of why someone would choose not to work.

2 Explain
a three benefits of specialisation in the workforce
b three drawbacks

of specialisation in the workplace.

3 List four different ways in which people may be paid.

4 Explain why a firm would pay overtime payments.

5 State three deductions that may appear on a pay slip.

6 Explain the difference between gross and net pay.

7 Identify three non-monetary factors that would affect the supply of labour.

8 Explain why the demand for labour is a derived demand.

9 State two reasons why women were traditionally less likely than men to supply their labour.

10 Give three factors that account for differences in the amount that different occupations pay.

11 Analyse the effect on wages of a shortage of labour in a particular industry.

12 Explain three costs to the individual of unemployment.

13 Give three strategies to help the long-term unemployed back into work.

3 National and global economy

Aims

✔ Understand international trade and its importance to the UK economy.

✔ Understand factors influencing international trade, including exchange rates and their impact on consumers' choices.

✔ Understand how global economies are influenced by consumer choice and government action.

✔ Understand how labour markets are affected by globalisation and migration.

This chapter introduces you to the national and global economy. It looks at international trade and the main types of goods and services which the UK trades internationally. Importing and exporting goods brings many advantages to the UK, but you will also find out that there are some disadvantages as well.

Exchange rate movements have a powerful impact on the volume of exports and imports, and also on the purchase decisions of individual citizens. They look at these and other factors that influence our decision to buy imports, and that affect the desirability of the UK's exports to foreign buyers.

We go on to see that as consumers we can influence producers. This chapter investigates the ways that consumers are using their buying power for goods, particularly for helping poorer producers in less developed countries. We look at the growth in popularity of 'Fairtrade' and ethical products. In addition, we see how the government plays its part in this by campaigning for issues like the reduction in world poverty.

The global economy also affects the UK's labour market and therefore jobs. Through the goods we buy, we influence the pattern of employment both in our own country and across the world. People can also choose to seek employment abroad with increasing ease, which creates large flows of migrant workers, particularly within the EU. We look at the positive and negative aspects of this (e.g. the unemployment and new employment possibilities in the labour market in the UK).

The UK trades a high value of goods and services with other countries each year. **Exports** are goods and services that the UK sells to buyers in foreign countries (e.g. Jaguar cars) and **imports** are the goods and services the UK buys from other countries (e.g. Volkswagen cars). 'Goods' are things like televisions or cameras, which can be physically handled, often called 'visibles'. 'Services' are things like tourism or insurance, which cannot be handled or seen, often called 'invisibles'.

The difference between the value of all the exports and all the imports is called the **balance of payments**. The table below shows the balance of payments for a selection of goods and services traded by the UK. The UK tends to import relatively more goods than it exports, while the opposite is true of services. As you can see, the UK has been particularly strong in exporting financial services.

Objectives

Learn the main types of UK export and import.

Appreciate the importance of trade to the UK economy.

Understand advantages and disadvantages of global trade and the UK's exports and imports.

Key terms

Exports: goods and services sold to another country.

Imports: goods and services bought from another country.

Balance of payments: a record of the value of a country's exports, imports and financial transactions with the rest of the world over the year.

A *UK balance of payments*

Goods	Exports £bn	Imports £bn	Net balance £bn
Food, beverages, tobacco	11,759	26,777	-15,018
Oil (crude + oil products)	22,749	26,796	-4,047
Semi-manufactured goods (chemicals + other)	68,222	74,517	-6,295
Cars	14,284	21,514	-7,230
Capital goods	29,825	41,388	-11,563
Finished manufactured goods – total	109,343	164,876	-55,533
Commodities	1,169	2,274	-1,105

*Source: Adapted from the **Pink Book** 2008*

Services	Exports £bn	Imports £bn	Net balance £bn
Transport	16,447	18,636	-2,189
Travel	18,826	36,158	-17,332
Insurance	5,529	1,016	4,513
Financial services	35,060	6,813	28,247

*Source: Adapted from the **Pink Book** 2008*

B *Examples of goods*

C *Examples of services*

Importance of trade to the UK economy

The UK accounted for the sixth largest share, 3.8 per cent, of the world's trade in goods in 2007, and the second largest share, 7.3 per cent, in the world's trade in **commercial services**.

International trade is extremely important to the UK economy, providing a large number of jobs. Each country has different raw materials, climates, cultures, labour skills, and so on, giving advantages in producing certain types of goods and services, known as a comparative advantage. The UK can specialise in producing the goods and services that it makes better and more efficiently than our competitors. The surplus goods are then sold abroad, creating jobs for UK citizens.

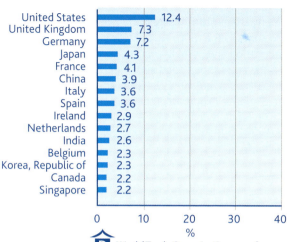

D *World Trade Organisation members % share in world commercial services trade, 2007*

E

	Exported	Imported	Balance
Total value of UK goods	£220,703bn	£309,955bn	−£89,252bn
Total value of UK services	£147,634bn	£105,862bn	£41,772bn
Overall balance of payments			−£47,480bn

Source: Adapted from the **Pink Book** *2008*

Advantages of trade to the UK economy

Globalisation is the name given to the process of increasing international trade and economic interdependence that has taken place in recent decades. It has made it easier to buy products produced around the world, and for UK producers to sell in other countries. Having access to so many goods and markets is bringing the UK many benefits, such as:

- income – increased production means more workers are needed, and this means more jobs.
- growth – growing exports mean increasing production, which leads to higher economic growth (i.e. the **GDP** will rise each year).
- choice and product differentiation – UK citizens can choose from goods not otherwise available in the UK.
- prices – many of the consumer goods we buy in the UK are imported from countries like China and India. These economies have much lower labour costs than the UK, and have relatively good levels of technology. They can therefore produce goods much more cheaply than UK manufacturers.
- competition and innovation – all companies have to work harder to attract consumers as there are many more potential competitors. They try to lower prices and develop more attractive and better quality products.
- raw materials – the UK is relatively poor in raw materials, so it is essential that we import the materials (metals, gems, energy, and so on) that we need.

Key terms

Commercial services: services which are used and supplied by businesses e.g. banking, training and transport.

Globalisation: the process of increasing international trade and economic interdependence between countries.

Gross Domestic Product (GDP): total value of goods and services produced by an economy in one year.

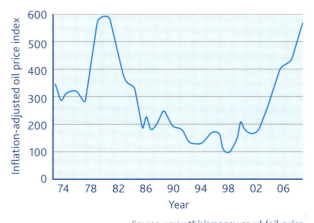

Many students from across the world pay large amounts to come to the UK to study English. The value of UK education and training exports is worth more than those of the automotive, food and drink, or financial services industries: a massive £28 billion compared with those for automotive exports (£20 billion), construction exports (£7 billion), food and drink exports (£9.4 billion), financial Services (£19 billion) and healthcare services exports (£14 billion).

Source: British Council report *Global Value – The Value of UK Education and Training Exports*, September 2007

Activities

1. Explain what is meant by an 'education and training export'.

2. Outline how and why the exports referred to above would help the UK economy.

3. Explain how education and training exports of £28bn could help create jobs for UK workers.

Disadvantages of trade to the UK economy

- Competition – increased competition may benefit consumers in terms of having cheaper goods and greater variety, but UK firms may find it difficult to compete. Many countries (e.g. the BRIC countries (Brazil, Russia, China and India)) have much lower labour costs than the UK, yet their workforces are relatively well trained.

- Economic dependency – for example, the UK imports a large variety of foods; interruption of this might threaten our survival.

- Unstable commodity prices – the prices of raw materials and foodstuffs can change by large amounts very quickly. This affects both production costs and the prices to consumers. This can have both good and bad effects.

- Power of MNCs – multinational corporations (MNCs) are becoming very powerful. All governments are finding it harder to control MNCs.

- Environment and sustainability – see opposite.

Source: www.thisismoney.co.uk/oil-price

F The UK is dependent on imported oil. Energy is needed to produce and distribute all kinds of goods. Oil price changes affect production costs

Activity

4. For each of the items shown, compare the possible products available when there is international trade with what would be available if there were *no* international trade.

G *Holidays*

H *Food*

I *Electrical products*

Social and environmental impact of trade

Although we might enjoy cheaper goods and better choice, much international trade carries a high price in terms of environmental impact. We call this impact the **carbon footprint**. You may already be familiar with this term, as many products – clothes, toys, cars – now carry a measurement of their carbon footprint.

The full carbon footprint of a product comes from a wide range of emissions sources:

- direct emissions of CO_2 – from activities the organisation controls (e.g. using energy for production, running a vehicle fleet)

- indirect emissions of CO_2 – the carbon that is emitted in the preparation and transport of the raw materials used, employee travel to work, and so on.

Adapted from the Carbon Trust website
www.carbontrust.co.uk

Goods bought from other countries inevitably require more energy to transport them, often over vast distances. This increases the CO_2 equivalent.

J *Even a packet of crisps may carry a calculation of its carbon footprint*

Key terms

Carbon footprint: the total greenhouse gas (CO_2 equivalent) emissions caused by an individual, event, organisation or product or good traded by the UK.

Case study

A Cranfield University study found that the carbon footprint of roses produced in Holland, which require a lot of artificial heat to make them grow, was over 5.8 times that of roses produced in Kenya, even after including the emissions from air freight. When they compared a field of green beans grown outdoors in the UK with beans from Kenya, the carbon footprint of the UK-grown beans was lower. The UK is over 4,000 miles from Kenya.

K *Rose farming in Kenya*

Activities

5 Explain what is meant by 'carbon footprint'.

6 Explain why the carbon footprint for roses grown in Holland is 5.8 times higher than for roses grown in Kenya.

7 Why do you think the carbon footprint for green beans grown in the UK is lower than for ones grown in Kenya?

8 Go to **www.carbontrust.co.uk/solutions/ CarbonFootprinting/FootprintCalculators** and try calculating your own carbon footprint.

AQA Examiner's tip

When you are explaining the carbon footprint of a product, be sure to include all the products and services that a firm uses, and transport of the finished goods.

■ Effect of exchange rates on imports and exports

Every time a UK citizen or business wants to buy something from abroad, they need to pay for that product in the currency of the country where it is produced. For an individual UK citizen, this is likely to be for a foreign holiday, or for buying expensive consumer goods directly from a foreign manufacturer (e.g. a car). The amount they have to pay for this currency depends on the **exchange rate**. For example:

- £1:$2 – every dollar we want to buy will cost £0.50. For an item imported from the US priced $10, a UK citizen will need to pay £5 to buy the dollars necessary.
- £1:$1 (the exchange rate of the pound has fallen) – every dollar we want to buy will cost £1. For an item imported from the US priced $10, a UK citizen will need to pay £10 to buy the dollars necessary.

The same is true when UK companies want to export goods and services. Foreign citizens need to buy pounds in order to pay for the goods.

- £1:$2 – every pound they want to buy will cost $2. For an item exported to the US priced £10, a US citizen will need to pay $20 to buy the pounds necessary.
- £1:$1 (the exchange rate of the dollar has risen) – every pound they want to buy will cost $1. For an item exported to the US priced £10, a US citizen will need to pay $10 to buy the pounds necessary.

Numerical examples of the impact of exchange rate changes

> 66 *Retailers near the Northern Irish and Republic of Ireland border can expect a bumper weekend after the pound fell to a record low against the euro for the third consecutive day.* 99
>
> Source: www.belfasttelegraph.co.uk, 12 December 2008

News articles like this clearly illustrate the effect that exchange rates have on imports and exports. At the time, the UK's currency, sterling, had fallen sharply against the euro. From the pound's all-time high of £1 = €1.75 in October 2000, it had, by December 2008, fallen to the level of £1 = €1.14. If you want to buy some euros, you will now have to pay £0.88 each for them, as opposed to £0.57 in October 2000. This affects imports and exports of goods and services into and out of the UK.

Objectives

Understand how exchange rates influence demand for imports and exports of goods and raw materials.

Understand non-price **factors** affecting demand for imports to and exports from the UK.

Key terms

Exchange rates: the rate at which one currency exchanges for another.

Factors affecting sales of exports and imports: things that influence consumers to buy imports/exports, other than price.

A *Exchange rates can change daily*

Possible effects of exchange rates on exports

Shoppers from the Republic of Ireland, who use the euro as their currency, found that Christmas shopping in Northern Ireland just got cheaper (as Northern Ireland uses the pound)! Compared with October 2000, £100 worth of goods purchased in Northern Ireland in December 2008 changed as follows:

October 2000	£100/0.57 = €175.43
December 2008	£100/0.88 = €113.63

Many goods and services which the UK exports to the 'eurozone' will now cost less in euros. This will make them more attractive to many European buyers. The cost of UK goods to people who use the euro has fallen by 35 per cent. Exports from Northern Ireland look set to increase!

Travel to the UK will now be cheaper. This is likely to encourage people from the 'eurozone' to take holidays in the UK, rather than other places in the world. While they are here, they will find our goods and services cheaper to buy, so will probably buy more of these as well. All these influences will help to increase UK exports, jobs, income and growth.

B UK products for export – cheaper in 2009 than before

Effect of exchange rates on imports

> ❝ *The weakness of sterling is lending crucial support to the UK farming economy, helping to boost export earnings while protecting the industry from lower-priced imports.* ❞
>
> Source: www.fwi.co.uk, 12 December 2008

The falling pound also has the effect of raising import prices. The UK farming industry was very pleased about the fall in the value of the pound at the end of 2008 as we can see from the above. It helps them in two ways:

- Firstly, the weaker pound helps the farmers to export their produce abroad, by making their goods cheaper.
- Secondly, it makes imported foodstuffs from the 'eurozone' (meat, fruit and vegetables) more expensive. This makes the UK-produced meat, fruit and vegetables relatively cheap for UK citizens to buy, so buyers in the UK buy these goods and not the imported ones. This helps boost incomes for UK farmers.

On the other hand, it is going to be much more expensive for holders of the pound (e.g. UK citizens) to buy goods or services priced in euros.

October 2000	€100/1.75 = £57.14
December 2008	€100/1.36 = £73.53

Many goods and services which the UK imports from the 'eurozone' will now cost more in pounds. This will make them less attractive to many UK buyers, who may buy UK-produced goods instead. The cost of 'eurozone' goods to people who use the pound has risen by 29 per cent. Imports from the 'eurozone' are set to fall!

Exchange rates and the individual consumer

Individual consumers are affected by changes in exchange rates in the same way. A consumer thinking of buying a new imported car, or taking a foreign holiday, should find the price reduced when the pound appreciates, and vice versa. This will influence the type of goods and services which you buy because their prices will change.

When you exchange pounds for other currencies, the amount of foreign currency you receive will also be affected by the value of the pound. If the value of the pound appreciates, you will receive more foreign currency, which will allow you to spend more when you go abroad, effectively making your holiday cheaper. The reverse is also true.

Overall UK consumers will find the cost of the following types of good are affected directly by changes in the exchange rate of the pound:

- foreign holidays
- withdrawing cash from cash machines abroad
- food in supermarkets
- imported consumer goods
- direct imports of big-ticket items like cars and furniture.

In addition, the production costs of anything produced from imported raw materials will also fall as the exchange rate rises. This could lead to lower prices, even of goods made in the UK. When the exchange rate falls, the opposite is true.

C Exchange rate changes affect the prices of things we buy abroad

USA Approx. number of US $ that one GBP (£) will buy: May 2007 £1 = $2 May 2009 £1 = $1.5	Average price in £ May 2007	Average price in £ May 2009	Japan Approx. number of Japanese Yen (JPY) that one GBP (£) will buy: May 2007 £1 = Y 239 May 2009 £1 = Y 148	Average price in £ May 2007	Average price in £ May 2009
Can of coke – $0.80	£0.40	£0.53	Can of coke - 140 JPY	£0.59	£0.95
Factor 15 suncream - $18	£9.00	£12.00	Factor 15 suncream - 2400 JPY	£10.04	£16.21
Bottle of beer - $3.50	£1.75	£2.33	Bottle of beer – 700 JPY	£2.93	£4.73

Source: author's own material

Activities

Phil and Polly planned a holiday to Australia six months ago. When they booked it, the exchange rate was £1: AUD 0.50 and the cost in Australian dollars was AUD 1,000. Since then the value of the pound has fallen sharply. The holiday must be paid for on arrival, in AUDs.

1 Calculate the cost of the holiday in pounds if the exchange rate is

a £1: AUD 0.50

b £1: AUD 0.40

2 When Phil and Polly first planned the holiday, they budgeted to spend £75 per day. By how much would that need to increase due to the fall in exchange rate?

3 Advise on the holiday options open to them, and how each one would affect the UK's imports and exports, if chosen by them.

Other factors that affect the sales of imports and exports

The exchange rate, via its effect on prices, is not the only influence on demand for imports and exports. Other factors include:

- style and image
- quality
- reliability.

BMWs are a prime example of a good that is expensive but that people still want to buy because of its quality and style. Fine wines and champagne from France, caviar from Russia, gemstones and high fashion are similar examples. Oil is something on which the UK depends and demands – price makes little difference to the amount the UK imports in the short term.

D *Some products are imported for their fine quality*

> **AQA** *Examiner's tip*
>
> Remember, exchange rates (price) are not the only thing that determines whether or not we buy imported products, or whether foreigners buy our exports.

Case study

'Travelling to Europe two weeks ago, I handed over £60 cash at the bureau de change in Luton airport. I was surprised when the cashier said he could give me €60 if I gave him another 65p' (a rate of £1 : €1.01).

That was the experience of Times Online's Gareth Scurlock, who says he'll be avoiding the 'eurozone' until the exchange rate improves.

Source: Timesonline, 10 December 2008

> **Activities**
>
> **4** Why do you think Gareth will be 'avoiding the "eurozone" until the exchange rate improves'?
>
> **5** Gareth also wants to buy an imported Audi car, costing €35,000. Calculate how much this would cost at an exchange rate of
>
> a £1 : €1.01
>
> b £1 : €1.4
>
> **6** Explain why Gareth might still prefer to buy the Audi, even at the lower exchange rate of the pound.

3.3 The power of the consumer

The power of consumers to influence producers and their products

Consumers can wield a large influence over producers. Through their buying choices, consumers can almost force producers to adapt their products to their demands. Consumer **boycotts** are becoming more common, and this is a result of **consumer empowerment**.

Consumers also demand cheaper products, so several UK manufacturers have moved their production facilities abroad to low labour-cost countries in order to compete with cheap imports. Producers responded to consumer demand for cheaper imported products.

Case study

A wide range of British industries (including textiles, electronics and toys) have all moved their manufacturing bases outside of the UK. Marks & Spencer, for example, was one of the last British clothing companies to shift the bulk of its manufacturing abroad. 'Globalisation was a fact of life that wasn't going away', said a Marks & Spencer spokeswoman.

Source: Adapted from http://news.bbc.co.uk/1/hi/business/1806463.stm

Activities

1. Research one or more companies that have decided to start manufacturing in cheaper countries than the UK in recent years.

2. Explain why a company might want to do this.

3. Why might Marks & Spencer or Hornby find it easier to move their production to a low labour-cost country than say Rolls-Royce or Aviva insurance?

An increasing number of people now read online product reviews, with up to 69 per cent of them passing on the information to friends or colleagues, making their impact greater.

Clearly, the consumer is becoming increasingly influential in the type of products that producers are supplying.

Firms on the other hand (through marketing and advertising) can also influence and shape consumer demands. Persuasive advertising is a powerful tool in their hands. There are also physical and financial limits on what firms can produce profitably, so the consumer does not have total control over the products on sale.

Objective

Understand that consumers have buying power and that this can be used to influence businesses to supply goods that are ethically sound.

Key terms

Boycott: to stop buying or using a product as a protest, to force a company to do, or stop doing, a particular action.

Consumer empowerment: consumers demonstrating their needs, wants and demands through their purchase decisions in the marketplace.

> " …in the past, clever advertisers shaped brands, but now consumers have a more powerful voice, and their opinions are spread almost instantly. "
>
> *Pat Conroy, vice-chairman and US consumer products group leader at Deloitte & Touche USA LLP. Adapted from www.marketingcharts.com*

A *The internet has given consumers a more powerful voice*

The individual's influence on the products businesses supply

The next time you are in a supermarket, look out for Fairtrade products that have this label (right).

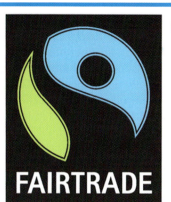

The Fairtrade movement aims to help poorer producers in developing countries gain economic self-sufficiency by encouraging the payment of fair prices for products such as coffee, cocoa and fresh fruit. High-street names such as Tesco and Marks & Spencer now stock Fairtrade products because of consumer pressure. Consumers are prepared to pay a premium to ensure that suppliers from less developed countries receive a fair deal. Marks & Spencer is now looking to stock an even bigger range of Fairtrade products because it has received such positive feedback from customers.

> **AQA Examiner's tip**
> The focus for Economics is that shops have adopted Fairtrade products because consumers demand them.

Case study

A study by media agency MPG UK found 70 per cent of UK families would support boycotting companies that don't take real steps to reduce their environmental impact.

Source: www.ethicalconsumer.org

Activities

4   Explain what you understand by the term 'boycott'.

5   Outline the steps that a car company might take in the light of this case study.

6   Research on the internet to find a selection of products that have been recently boycotted.

As consumers, we have buying power. Our buying habits influence what producers supply. We can even refuse to buy environmentally irresponsible products (e.g. those with excessive packaging). Companies fear mass consumer boycotts because it causes bad publicity and decreases sales.

Case study

B   *Bluefin tuna is an example of a product that it is environmentally irresponsible to buy or stock*

The environmental group, WWF, has called on global supermarket chains to take bluefin tuna off their shelves, saying overfishing, driven by the craze for sushi, threatens to wipe out the species. The French supermarket giant, Auchan, has already stopped selling bluefin tuna.

Source: www.ethicalconsumer.org

Activities

7   List the types of action that consumers could take to show supermarkets that they do not want them to stock environmentally irresponsible products like bluefin tuna.

8   How significant do you think consumers' opinions were in Auchan's decision to withdraw bluefin tuna from its shelves?

C   *… or eat*

As a consumer, you can make a real difference to the environmental sustainability of food production in the UK and globally, by what you choose to buy in supermarkets. Because of consumer demand, Tesco, Asda, Sainsbury's and Morrisons all say they are committed to sourcing foods locally where possible. This is important because it greatly cuts down the transport needed, therefore the pollution is reduced. It also helps to support local jobs in industries like farming, boosting the local economy.

A spokeswoman for Sainsbury's said that it was

> **"** aware that many of our customers want to buy local produce … We are committed to giving our customers the diverse range of local foods they want'. **"**

Source: Adapted from http://news.bbc.co.uk/1/hi/business/4316207.stm

Companies operate to generate profit, so **MNCs** sometimes set up sweatshop factories in developing countries, which have low operating costs. Typically sweatshops pay very low wages, have poor working conditions, long working hours, and hire young children.

Many consumers question whether it is right that we should be able to wear cheap clothes, for example, while the person who made them cannot afford to feed their children. Consumers can protest by refusing to buy products from MNCs that rely upon sweatshop production, showing that they care about these workers. Boycotting makes the large corporations sit up and listen, and hopefully change their ways. Consumers are powerful!

Source: Adapted from http://elektric-kat.blogspot.com/2005/03/why-we-should-boycott-sweatshop-labour.html

Activities

9 Why do you think Sainsbury's is so committed to providing locally produced food?

10 Analyse the advantages and disadvantages of consumers insisting on locally grown food.

11 Carry out research to find out at least four products in your local supermarket that are locally sourced.

Key terms

MNC: multinational corporation.

∞ links

www.coopamerica.org

D Cuetzalan boy spreading coffee beans to dry in Mexico. Children in some countries work long hours for very low pay

E Protests like these can raise awareness and persuade consumers to change their shopping habits

Case study

Co-op America publishes the 'Guide to Ending Sweatshops', which lists shoes, clothing, rugs and coffee as products that are often made in sweatshops. It ranks companies on a ladder scale of good to bad practices. It wants consumers to rethink their buying habits and make changes accordingly.

Source: Adapted from http://findarticles.com/p/articles/mi_qa5378/is_/ai_n21478788

Activities

12 What do you understand by a 'sweatshop'?

13 Explain why Co-op America thinks it important to give buyers information about sweatshop products.

14 Assess the likelihood that Co-op America will manage to stamp out sweatshop goods by providing this guide.

◻ The UK Government's role in reducing world poverty

The UK Government is one of the foremost governments working to rid the world of extreme poverty. The Department for International Development (DFID) is the part of the UK Government that manages Britain's aid to poor countries. It works to:

- eradicate extreme poverty and hunger
- achieve universal primary education
- ensure environmental sustainability.

These form part of the eight internationally agreed Millennium Development Goals (MDGs) to be met by 2015.

The government are doing this by tackling the causes of poverty such as; settling conflicts, increasing trade etc. Aid is also given directly to foreign governments of poor countries.

DFID is particularly committed to making international trade work for poor countries. Richer countries' wealth is built on the large choice of markets they can sell to – or buy from. The DFID works to get richer countries to play fair by allowing poorer countries to sell their products freely in Western markets, eg, by reducing import taxes on these goods, and works to get the West to pay fair prices.

∞ links

The DFID provides a guide to its trade development work called 'Trade Matters'. It can be downloaded free via the link:

www.dfid.gov.uk/tradematters

Research activity 🔍

15 Download the DFID guide 'Trade Matters' from **www.dfid.gov.uk/tradematters**. Using this and any other information available on the DFID website, write a brief report summarising the work the UK government is doing to help poorer countries to increase trade with the richer ones.

F *What do you understand by a 'sweatshop'?*

G *Helping to provide education – this DFID project in Somalia could help the country's economy to develop*

Understanding work in the national and global economy

Effects of globalisation on the UK labour market

Globalisation is effectively making the world a smaller place and is affecting the UK labour market. Workers are becoming internationally mobile, increasingly moving between countries to find work. In the European Union (EU), freedom to work in any EU country is guaranteed for most EU citizens.

Firms are also increasingly choosing to locate their factories abroad, often to take advantage of lower **labour costs** and production costs (e.g. to establish production plants in the former communist countries, China and India). A wide range of British industries (including textiles, electronics, toys and cars) have moved their manufacturing bases outside of the UK. Many UK companies, such as Vodafone and BP, derive the majority of their earnings from abroad.

> **Case study**
>
> Foreign companies have forced prices down by 50 per cent over seven years in electronics. Despite improving productivity, the chance of much lower labour costs in the Far East seemed to be the only way of substantially reducing overheads. 'You either take action or you watch your company fold', says Mr Cripwell, former managing director of an electrical appliances firm.
>
> *Source: Adapted from **http://news.bbc.co.uk***

Advantages to firms of operating overseas

- There are lower operating and labour costs.
- Firms have increased competitiveness.
- Exchange rates – if the exchange rate falls it lowers export prices.
- Firms are nearer to markets and/or sources of materials – reducing transport and distribution costs.

> **Case study**
>
> In 1999, about half of Marks & Spencer's clothes were supplied by manufacturers in the UK. Now the majority are imported from North Africa and Eastern Europe. Sourcing more clothes from abroad was a key factor in helping Marks & Spencer tackle its rising financial problems and dwindling high-street popularity.
>
> *Source: **http://news.bbc.co.uk***

Disadvantages of firms operating overseas

- Jobs are lost in the UK.
- Difficulty in controlling operations.
- Unfamiliar cultures and languages.
- Transport costs to home markets – can vary with the oil price.
- Exchange rate changes – changes can go against you, making trading more expensive and reducing profits from overseas factories.

Objectives

Understand the positive and negative effects of globalisation on the UK labour market.

Understand the nature of migration and its impact on the UK labour market.

Key terms

Labour costs: costs of employing workers (e.g. wages, salaries, taxes on labour) and also training and recruitment costs.

■ Why foreign firms choose to operate in the UK

The UK is one of the top economies in the world for **foreign direct investment**, holding over 20 per cent of all the inward investment stock in the 27 EU countries. Foreign companies can either set up factories in the UK or take over existing UK companies. Tata Steel, the Indian conglomerate, took over Corus Steel in 2007, then Jaguar and Land Rover in 2008. The Spanish bank Santander took over the Abbey and Alliance and Leicester banks in the same year.

Key terms

Foreign direct investment: when a business from one country builds a factory in another.

A   *UK companies recently acquired by foreign companies*

Sector	UK company	Acquiring company & country	Value added
Beverages	Allied Domecq	Pernod Ricard, France	£965m
Chemicals	BOC	Linde, Germany	£1781m
Construction	Pilkington	NSG, Japan	£1117m
	BPB	Saint-gobain, France	£827m
	Novor	Honeywell, US	£537m
Food producers	Geest	Bakkavor, Iceland	£266m
General retail	Body Shop Intl	L'Oreal, France	£171m
Industrial transport	BAA	Grupo Ferrovial, Spain	£1778m
	P&O	DP World, UAE	£576m
Support services	Brambles	Brambles, Australia	£964m

B   *Example of a UK company recently acquired by a foreign company*

Reasons why foreign firms locate in the UK:

- high-skilled labour force and higher quality production
- tariff-free access to the European Single Market (500 million consumers)
- to buy existing UK-owned brands and distribution networks
- the English language is the accepted international language of business, science and technology.

When foreign firms or MNCs decide to close a plant, however, there are problems for the UK economy:

- jobs are lost from the plant itself
- jobs are lost from other UK companies who supply the plant.

AQA *Examiner's tip*

The effects of a plant closure are almost never just on the workers in that factory. Always consider how workers in other companies might be affected.

Peugeot decided in 2006 to close its car plant near Coventry, to set up production in a country with lower labour costs. 2300 jobs were lost. Unions called it 'another nail in the coffin' of the UK's car industry. Nearly 6000 jobs were also lost the previous year at MG Rover in Birmingham. Many Peugeot components however are made outside the UK, so 'the ripple effect on the whole economy will not be as severe', said spokesman Alan Durham.

Source: Adapted from: **http://news.bbc.co.uk**

Activities

1. Outline the reasons that Peugeot decided to close its Coventry plant in 2006.

2. Explain why the unions used the phrase 'another nail in the coffin of the UK's car industry' to describe Peugeot's decision.

3. Evaluate the extent of possible 'ripple effects' on the UK economy, which closing this plant might have.

Case study

■ Globalisation and the mobility of labour

Globalisation is increasing the **mobility** of UK workers by offering them a growing variety of jobs abroad. The rising number of takeovers of UK companies by foreign firms, and vice versa, also increases the necessity for workers to work in many other countries around the globe.

The UK is a very **open economy**, so with globalisation it means regions dependent on low-skilled manufacturing may face unemployment, as production shifts to low labour-cost countries. On the other hand, regions offering high-skilled labour, or specialised services, may experience growth in employment, as new companies dependent on such skills relocate to the UK.

Case study

Sports car company TVR is to cease production in the UK, with the loss of 250 jobs at its factory in Blackpool.

TVR, which was bought by young Russian tycoon, Nikolai Smolensky, in 2004, said it was in consultation with unions over redundancies. Speculation that the firm would move production to another European country had been growing since the start of the year.

Source: Adapted from http://news.bbc.co.uk

Activities

4 Explain why a Russian tycoon might want to buy TVR.

5 Explain possible reasons why Smolensky might choose to relocate to another European country.

6 Explain how TVR's decision reflects some of the drawbacks of globalisation to the UK economy.

Benefits of globalisation for the UK labour market

- Jobs are created in sectors where the UK does well (e.g. financial services and highly specialised manufacturing).
- New migrant labour skills lower costs and increase competitiveness (e.g. skilled Polish plumbers emigrating to the UK eased a severe shortage of these skills in this country).
- There are opportunities to increase exports to new markets.

Drawbacks of globalisation for the UK labour market

- Low-skill jobs are lost, particularly affecting manufacturing regions of the UK.
- Increase in immigrant labour depresses wages.
- Relocating production overseas can cause unemployment (e.g. Marks & Spencer sourcing its clothes from overseas).

Impact of migration on the UK economy

Multinational corporations are businesses that operate in more than one country, and therefore create new job opportunities across the globe. Workers naturally **migrate** to where wages are highest, both within their own country and internationally. Because it is now easier to work abroad, large flows of migrant workers have been formed, particularly within the EU, where big wage differences between some member countries exist.

Immigration affects the UK labour market positively by:

- bringing new knowledge and skills, and filling gaps in the labour market (e.g. Polish plumbers)
- reducing wage inflation and increasing competitiveness
- providing more workers to support the UK's ageing population
- increasing the number of consumers as well as producers.

But increases in immigrant labour:

- depresses wages, and can displace low-skilled UK workers
- increases strain on social services, education and hospitals.

Emigration can affect the UK labour market by:

- losing valuable skills/human capital – the 'brain drain'
- reducing unemployment in recessions.

Despite increasing opportunities, some barriers remain to working abroad. These include:

- language and cultural barriers
- visas, work permits, and so on, are needed outside the EU
- restrictions by foreign governments.

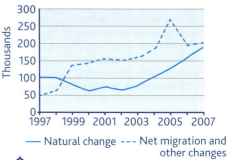

C Net migration into the UK 1997–2007

Source: *www.statistics.gov.uk*

The UK's immigration deal with Belgium

The UK has a deal with Belgium to place British immigration officials at the Brussels Eurostar train terminal to stop people boarding a train if they have no legal reason to enter the UK. The UK has also invested heavily in hi-tech scanning systems at ports in France, Belgium and Holland to detect those who may be hiding in lorries.

Source: *http://news.bbc.co.uk*

Activities

9 Explain why the UK government might want to limit the number of immigrant workers coming to the UK.

10 Outline reasons why the government thinks it important to allow agricultural immigrant labour to work in the UK.

11 Explain why the UK government takes such measures to restrict the number of immigrants to the UK.

In 2001, an estimated 70 per cent of catering jobs in London were filled by migrants. A year earlier, 40 per cent of hospitality firms had reported recruitment difficulties.

Source: *www.fastfoodjobs.co.uk*

Activities

7 What benefits might the UK catering industry obtain from employing so many immigrant workers?

8 Outline possible reasons why so many immigrant workers choose to work in the UK's catering industry.

Government action to regulate labour migration

The UK government regulates the flow of migration by:

- a points system – potential immigrants score points according to how well their skills match those needed by the UK
- the SAWS (Seasonal Agricultural Workers Scheme), which allows farmers and growers to bring foreign persons to the UK to do seasonal and agricultural work.

AQA Examiner's tip

The exam may call for you to explain economic reasons for restricting immigration (e.g. insufficient gaps in the labour market).

Chapter summary

3

By now you should have a clear understanding of:

✔ the advantages and disadvantages of global trade and its importance to the UK economy

✔ the main types of UK export and import

✔ how exchange rates and other factors influence demand for imports and exports

✔ consumer buying power, which can be used to encourage ethically sound production

✔ government actions to help poorer countries

✔ the positive and negative effects of globalisation and migration on the UK labour market.

Revision quiz

1 Choose true/false/maybe. Firms trade overseas because:

a No markets for the products exist in the UK (true/false/maybe)

b Goods can be exported more easily when the value of the pound is high. (true/false/maybe)

2 Circle true/false/maybe. Globalisation is good for the UK economy because:

a It opens up the chance to sell UK products in more markets. (true/false/maybe)

b It means consumers will buy more ethically produced products. (true/false/maybe)

c Unemployment will fall because more jobs are created. (true/false/maybe)

d We can buy imported products much more cheaply. (true/false/maybe)

3 Which answer is correct? Consumer power is most effective in promoting ethical production by:

a consumers' choices ensuring that goods are produced in the lowest-cost countries?

b consumers choosing to buy goods known to be produced under fair and ethical conditions?

c consumers choosing more expensive goods, which means that suppliers can be paid more?

d consumers always choosing to buy locally made produce?

4 What is the difference between an export and an import?

5 What is meant by the term 'balance of payments'?

6 In 2007, where did the UK rank in size of

a trade in goods   b trade in commercial services?

7 Explain the effect that the UK's high export of goods and services would have on jobs.

8 State two advantages and two disadvantages to the UK of a high level of international trade.

9 Explain what is meant by a person's or product's 'carbon footprint'.

10 Analyse why internationally traded goods might have a high 'carbon footprint'.

11 Outline why shops like Tesco and Marks & Spencer increasingly stock 'Fairtrade' goods.

12 Calculate the price in pounds of a restaurant meal in France costing €30, if the value of the euro is: a £0.65   b   £0.95

13 Outline the effects a 20 per cent rise in the value of the pound might have on the goods/services you would buy.

14 List two things, other than the exchange rate, that would influence your choice to buy an imported good or service.

15 Briefly outline how the government is trying to eradicate world poverty.

16 Explain three reasons why a business might choose to set up in the UK.

17 List two benefits and two drawbacks of globalisation for the UK labour market.

18 Explain why the government might want to limit the number of immigrant workers coming to the UK.

4 Managing the economy

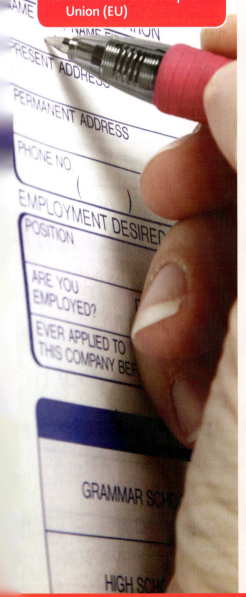

Aims

✔ Understand what the government's economic objectives are.

✔ Understand how the economic objectives are measured.

✔ Understand why economic growth is important and how it relates to ethics.

✔ Understand what the welfare state is and its alternatives.

✔ Understand how the economy works and how it fails.

✔ Understand what policies the government uses for managing the economy.

✔ Understand the UK's membership of the European Union.

✔ Understand the case for and against joining the euro.

This chapter looks at how the economy operates on a national basis. This means we look at the economy of the country as a whole. We examine some of the common economic problems that governments face. Governments have a number of different policies that they can use to solve some of these economic problems, such as interest rates and taxation, and we look at the effects of these policies.

We also look at how the UK is affected by European Union (EU) membership and at the benefits and drawbacks of membership. The likely effects for consumers and businesses of EU expansion are examined and the case for and against joining the single European currency (the euro) is also considered.

4.1   Economic objectives of the government

■ Economic objectives

Objectives are aims that the government would like to achieve. Governments have **economic objectives** for the whole economy, objectives it feels would be beneficial for the people and the country as a whole if they are achieved. The UK government will be judged partly by how well it manages to achieve these objectives. There are a variety of economic objectives the government aims for as follows:

- economic growth
- full employment
- stable prices
- balance of payments.

Economic growth

Economic growth looks at how fast national income grows over a period of time. This is normally measured over one year, although the data in the UK is also calculated on a quarterly basis.

Governments want economic growth to be high because high growth adds to national income, which leads to higher incomes and a better standard of living for the population. However, problems are encountered when economic growth is too high, which may lead to problems in achieving other economic objectives. For example, a feature of high growth is high consumer spending and this is often a cause of rising prices which conflicts with the objective of achieving stable prices.

Full employment

Unemployment refers to those of working age who are not currently working and are not in full-time education. Governments want to achieve **full employment**. This does not mean the same as zero unemployment. Full employment is achieved when those who are actively looking for employment can find employment. If unemployment falls below the full employment level, this means more workers have incomes available to spend, which can often lead to rising prices, which, again, conflicts with other economic objectives.

Stable prices

The government would prefer that prices are generally stable (i.e. that prices neither rise nor fall). This does not mean that no prices change at all, but that the average level of prices is stable. A period when prices are continually rising is known as inflation.

Activity

2   Look at the inflation report on the Bank of England's website. What does the Bank of England think will happen to inflation over the next two years?

Objectives

Understand what the economic objectives of the government are.

Understand why these objectives are important.

Understand how ethics affect the government's objectives.

Understand how economic indicators in the UK are measured.

Key terms

Economic objectives: economic goals.

Economic growth: the percentage change in national income measured over time.

Full employment: where all those seeking work are in employment.

Activity

1   What reasons may there be for a person not being in employment?

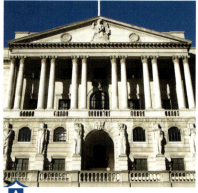

A *The Bank of England in Threadneedle Street*

 links

www.bankofengland.co.uk

Balance of payments

The balance of payments refers to financial transactions between the UK and all other foreign countries over a period of time. The government would prefer to see the balance of payments at a level where the value of exports is equal to imports – where the traded element of the balance of payments is equal. This is because if the value of imports is higher than the value of exports, then more money will be leaving the country than is flowing in – and this will mean savings are spent, or more borrowing is needed by the government, to finance these higher imports. However, this is only a major problem if the gap between imports and exports is high and continues to be high for a number of years.

How ethical issues affect the achievement of government objectives

Ethics refer to an informal code of how we should behave – decisions we all make about what is morally right or morally wrong. This code is often based on principles such as fairness.

The UK government believes that it is ethically right to aim to minimise poverty. The government also aims to minimise income inequality – where incomes are too spread out and the gap between rich and poor is too wide.

The main strategy to minimise poverty and to reduce income inequality is through the tax and welfare benefits system, where those with high incomes pay a higher proportion of their incomes as tax, which can help finance the benefit payments to those on lower incomes. This is done because the government believes that equality is a fairer outcome – though the government does not want income to be distributed completely equally. Distributing income equally would mean taxes would need to be raised on the higher earners, which would be unpopular and would probably remove the incentive for people to strive for higher earnings. If you knew the government would ensure all incomes were equal, what incentives would there be for working longer hours?

Activity

3   Look online at the government's data on foreign trade. List the major industries contributing to UK exports.

links

Government statistics website
www.statistics.gov.uk

B *The gap between the richest and the poorest: how wide should it be?*

UK key economic statistics for 2002–7

C

Year	Unemployment (% of workforce)	GDP (% growth)	Inflation (% change over year)
2002	5.3	2.1	1.3
2003	5.2	2.8	1.4
2004	4.9	2.8	1.3
2005	5.0	2.1	2.1
2006	5.6	2.8	2.3
2007	5.5	3.0	2.3

Source: ONS www.statistics.gov.uk

Activity

4   Based on the UK key economic statistics for 2002–7, state when the government came closest to meeting its objectives. Justify your answer.

Case study

4.2 Economic growth and ethical issues

Why is economic growth important?

Economic growth is an objective because significant benefits are gained from growth. However, governments also have an ethical element to their actions. The government aims to improve living standards, but also aims for an amount of **equality**. This means that it may aim to redistribute some income from those earning large amounts to those less fortunate.

Benefits of growth

Higher living standards

Higher growth means higher incomes for the population. It may not affect each person in the same way but growth means that people can buy more and generally enjoy a higher standard of living.

Reduction of poverty

Economic growth helps to move poorer sections of the population out of poverty by providing opportunities for better living standards. Historically, economic growth has allowed many citizens to escape poverty. **Absolute poverty** has been eliminated in the UK, but **relative poverty** still exists.

Investments in infrastructure

Higher growth means that governments collect more tax revenue and therefore can afford to spend more on priority areas, such as:

- improving education provision and encouraging access to education for more of the population
- providing improved health provision, including health education – the poorer sections of society tend to have more health problems
- improved transport links – greater investments in public transport and roads means that the economy is also likely to grow faster in future years.

Lower crime

There appears to be a link between economic growth and levels of crime. As growth rises, some crimes (e.g. property crimes) fall as the incentive to commit crime is reduced.

Costs of growth

Higher economic growth is desirable but there are drawbacks to having a growing economy.

Environmental costs

Higher growth means higher output. This may have negative effects. For example, higher factory output often generates higher pollution. Other problems of high growth also emerge, such as worsening traffic congestion and unaffordable house prices (see 4.4).

A *More factory input can mean more pollution*

Inequality

Although growth is beneficial, all won't benefit equally. It is most likely that those benefiting greatest are already earning above average incomes. Those with below average incomes often find incomes largely unchanged. This income inequality may lead to a significant part of the population falling into 'relative' poverty, where incomes are low relative to the rest of the country.

The government attempts to reduce the gap between rich and poor through the welfare state.

Activities

1 Describe what has broadly happened to the income share of the top and bottom 20 per cent of the population over the last 30 years.

2 Does this mean that we are reducing income inequality?

3 What measures could the government take to reduce income inequality?

■ Conflicts with other economic objectives

Government economic objectives are usually hard to achieve simultaneously. Achieving the objective of high growth can conflict with two other economic objectives, low inflation and balance of payments.

Low inflation

High growth is likely to lead to higher inflation because growth and spending are closely linked. Higher spending often leads to rising prices throughout the economy. This is because higher growth means resources in the economy (such as workers and the factories and machinery used for production) are more fully used and become scarcer, which leads to the prices of resources (and the goods produced) increasing.

Balance of payments

Higher growth leads to higher consumer expenditure and this means more imports are purchased. This leads to the current account section moving close to, or into, a trade deficit. The only way in which this can be avoided is if the economic growth itself arises out of an increase in demand for our exports. The higher exports would not have the same negative impact on the balance of payments. However, in the UK, this type of export-led growth has rarely occurred.

Case study

Income inequality in the UK

The following chart shows the share of total disposable income earned by the richest 20% of the population, then the share earned by the next richest 20%, down to the share earned by the poorest 20% (each 20% of the population is known as a quintile). For example, the richest quintile earn around 40% of total UK income, whereas the poorest 20% earn slightly less than 10% of the total UK income.

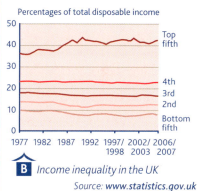

Percentages of total disposable income

B *Income inequality in the UK*

Source: www.statistics.gov.uk

AQA *Examiner's tip*

Don't confuse a fall in the rate of economic growth with negative economic growth.

∞ links

The UK site for statistics on poverty and social exclusion http://www.poverty.org.uk/

UK economic growth

This chart shows economic growth in the UK. It is measured both by the annual change (4q) and by the change over a three-month period (1q). Quarters (q) of the year are used as this is the time period for which economic growth data is calculated in the UK.

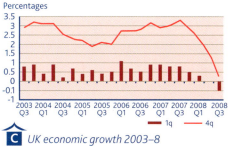

Percentages

C *UK economic growth 2003–8*

Source: www.statistics.gov.uk

Activities

4 In which quarter (1q) was growth **a** highest and **b** lowest?

5 Explain the drawbacks to the UK of experiencing high growth.

Case study

The welfare state and its alternatives

■ What is the welfare state?

The **welfare state** refers to various forms of benefit payments and services, designed to care for those who need support. In the UK, there are a number of benefits given to those in need. These benefits are funded by taxation revenue collected by government. The principle of this taxation is that those who earn higher than average incomes pay a greater proportion of their income as tax than those on below average incomes.

■ Benefits of the welfare state

Poverty is reduced

The welfare state provides support in the form of money transfers and other benefits, such as income support for the unemployed and a state retirement pension for those who have retired from work. This means that the poorest members of society avoid falling into absolute poverty.

Inequality is reduced

The welfare state is funded by the government taxing the population. Those with higher incomes provide more tax. This means that the richest proportion of the population is taxed more heavily, which provides income for the poorest proportion of the population and narrows the gap between richest and poorest. Reducing inequality is seen as ethically correct, but many also believe that societies with a more equal distribution of income suffer fewer social problems, like crime.

Overall health of population is increased

We all benefit from the welfare state – through universal access to health care and education. The NHS provides health care and medical treatment free of charge for all (apart from prescription charges). If health care was left solely to private firms to provide, those on lower incomes might not receive the full benefits of the health care and may not, as a result, enjoy the same level of health.

The health of the population is linked with income. Therefore, the welfare state improves the health of the poorer segments of the population in particular, as they receive money transfers.

■ Costs of the welfare state

Removal of incentives to find work

Some people think that providing the unemployed with benefit payments removes incentive to find employment. This is because the benefits received will, in some cases, almost provide the same income as from low-paid jobs. Therefore, it is possible that some unemployed prople will not search for jobs as urgently as if there was no benefit.

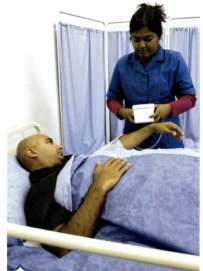

A *The NHS: free healthcare at the point of delivery*

Higher taxation

Those in employment, especially on average and above-average incomes, find that they are paying a higher proportion of their incomes in taxes than if there was no welfare state. Some argue that it is unfair to make those who are making high contributions to the nation's income pay higher taxes.

Activities

1 What reasons are there for the UK government to want to reduce the proportion of the population in poverty?

2 Can we ever eliminate relative poverty? Explain your answer.

▮ Alternatives to the welfare state

All political parties support the idea of the welfare state. However, some people argue that the welfare state could be reformed. Some alternative ideas are as follows:

Increase the role of the voluntary sector

The voluntary sector (also known as the charity sector) can contribute to providing support to those who rely on the welfare state. Charities and voluntary organisations employ over 500,000 workers in the UK. Famous charities, such as Oxfam and British Heart Foundation, raise money for particular concerns. There are also many small-scale charities that provide support for those without jobs or homes.

Modify the welfare state

Some argue that the welfare state should continue to exist but could be changed as follows:

Make benefits universal

Some benefits are paid out regardless of the income of those receiving the benefit. Child benefits are paid to the all families with children. This could be applied to all benefits. It would be easier to administer but may cost more in total.

Have benefits only for those meeting certain conditions

This would mean that only those who needed the benefits would receive them. Although this may seem as though it would save money, there would be a need for costlier administration to find out who meets the conditions for the benefits.

Poverty

The chart below shows the proportion of the population for each country that would be considered to be in relative poverty.

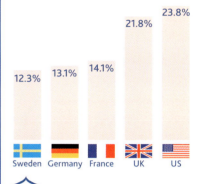

Sweden 12.3% · Germany 13.1% · France 14.1% · UK 21.8% · US 23.8%

B *Percentage of population living below 60% of average income*

Source: Luxembourg Income Study (LIS) Key figures, **http://www.lisproject.org/** (website visited Jan 2009)

C *A member of the Salvation Army caring for a homeless person*

4.4 The economy at work

Types of economy

Economic systems

The main economic systems which exist are:

- free-market economies
- mixed economies.

Free-market economies

Under this system, economic activity occurs through private businesses and private individuals. Businesses exist to make a profit for their owners and they will produce whatever maximises profits.

Competition between businesses helps to keep prices sufficiently low and the quality of goods high. Businesses failing to provide goods of sufficient quality or at a sufficiently low price will lose out to other firms.

Consumers can buy whatever they want if they have enough income. If not, they will go without.

Governments still exist but will be mainly concerned with ensuring that laws are complied with.

Benefits of a free-market economy

- Prices should be lower as competition between businesses ensures prices cannot rise too quickly.
- Quality of output should be high, also due to competition.

Drawbacks of a free-market economy

- Some businesses may monopolise a market and will not have to provide low prices and high quality due to the lack of competition.
- Consumers may not be able to afford vital products – especially if they cannot provide for themselves, meaning that poverty and inequality are more likely.

Mixed economies

Mixed economies operate similarly to free-market economies. However, governments participate in the mixed economy. Governments provide certain services seen as vital for the economy, such as health and education. If these services were left to the free market, people may not be able to afford them and could miss out on vital services.

Objectives

Understand the differences between free-market and mixed economies.

Understand how markets can fail.

Understand how positive and negative externalities arise.

Understand the stages and features of the economic cycle.

Key terms

Free-market economy: a system where all economic decisions are taken by private individuals and businesses.

Mixed economy: a system that is partly a free-market economy but also has government involvement in economic decisions.

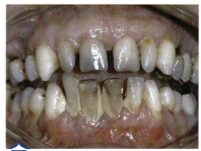

A *If dental services are left to a free market, people may not be able to afford them*

Activity

1 In the 1980s, many government-owned enterprises were transferred to the private sector. List four businesses in the UK that were once owned by the government.

All developed countries operate as mixed economies. The balance between private businesses and the government differs between countries. For example, European governments have a more active role in the economy than in the US. However, even in Europe, there are variations on how much a government participates in the economy – with the UK government less likely to be involved than certain other countries.

Market failure

What is meant by market failure?

A market is an arrangement for which a buyer and seller can conduct a transaction together. Markets left to operate freely have a good chance of operating efficiently. By operating efficiently, business costs can be kept low in order to improve profits. In this way, the market ensures that the resources are allocated efficiently.

Market failure occurs when markets fail to allocate resources efficiently. This means that the prices of goods and the quantities produced are not at the level that ensures that economic welfare is kept as high as possible. For example, if a market fails, some goods may be under-produced or not even produced at all.

How can markets fail?

There are a number of reasons why markets can fail. Externalities are covered later. Other ways in which markets fail are:

Lack of competition

Less competition in a market means a greater risk of market failure. This is because the lack of competition leads to inefficiencies in how businesses operate. With little or no competition, there is less incentive for firms to improve the quality of output and to keep prices low. For example, it was only after several 'discount' airlines (such as Ryanair and easyJet) began to compete with more established airlines, that flight prices fell.

Not all our values are market values

Some types of goods are valued differently by society than the monetary value placed on them by the market. **Merit goods** and services are those that are not produced in sufficient quantities in a free market. Education and healthcare in the UK would not be produced in sufficient quantity by a free market because consumers would not want to purchase enough of these services. This is because individuals may not have enough knowledge to assess the true **private benefits** that consuming a particular product would generate. For example, we might not understand the true social benefits of having adequate healthcare provision if we had to purchase it as a normal service. As a result, the government steps in and ensures that these are provided for consumers by providing healthcare free of charge through the National Health Service or using the law to enforce schooling.

Activity

2 Look online to see which governments in the EU spend the greatest amount in relation to the size of the economy.

Key terms

Market failure: a failure of the market to allocate resources efficiently.

Merit goods: goods that are under-consumed by society – largely because the benefits of the good are not fully appreciated by society.

Private benefit: the benefit to private businesses or individuals.

Demerit goods (on page 72): goods that are over-consumed by society. Negative externalities are generated by consumption of these goods.

B *Education is an example of merit goods*

There are goods known as **demerit goods,** which are generally over-provided by the market. Demand for these is high because individuals are not good at seeing the negative consequences of the consumption. Common examples of demerit goods are illegal drugs and tobacco.

Public goods would not be produced at all if the market was left to operate freely. This is because it would be very hard for businesses to generate any profit at all through the provision of public goods, because it is hard to stop people benefitting from their provision once given, thereby making it very hard to charge people for the service. People could still benefit from the service as long as someone else paid. Public goods are also goods that can be consumed by one person without this preventing someone else from consuming the public good at the same time. Examples of public goods are street lighting and the armed forces.

Activity

5 List examples of public goods currently provided in the UK, stating how they are financed.

■ Externalities

What are externalities?

Externalities exist when the costs of producing goods, and the benefits gained from consuming goods, don't match the true costs and benefits to society. For example, a business that pollutes the environment will only pay the costs of production and will not pay directly for the pollution it creates – this is a cost the rest of society has to pay in terms of dirty air and poisoned rivers. This pollution is an externality – it represents an external cost and is another form of market failure.

Negative externalities

Negative externalities occur when the cost to society exceeds the **private cost** to the business. The external cost is that paid by the rest of society. The negative externality does not result in an actual payment of money but society suffers from this external cost.

Negative externalities will mean that businesses produce higher levels of output than if they had to pay the full **social cost** (including the external cost) as well as the private cost.

Positive externalities

Positive externalities occur when the benefits to society from consumption of a product exceed the private benefits to the individual consumer. For example, the private benefits to a town of having a large business set up in the local area would include the business gaining extra profits but it would be the (local) society that gains from the external benefits of the new business in terms of the employment opportunities and the extra income generated.

Activities

3
  a List three goods or services that the UK government insists that we 'consume'.

  b Why do you think this is?

  c Are there any common features in these services?

4 If education is a merit good, explain why the government decided to charge tuition fees for the majority of those attending university.

Key terms

Public goods: goods that display the following two characteristics: consumption of them doesn't prevent others consuming them; once they are provided, people cannot be prevented from consuming them.

Externalities: the additional costs or benefits beyond private ones imposed on society that arise out of a production or consumption decision.

Private cost: the cost to private businesses or individuals.

Social cost: the cost to society of an action consisting of private costs and external costs.

Remember

social costs = private cost + external cost.

Activity

6 List all the external costs caused by the airline industry.

C

Examples of negative externalities	Examples of positive externalities
traffic congestion	increased numbers attending university
air pollution generated by burning of fossil fuels	employment opportunities for town of new business locating there
noise generated from building site	pleasure from interesting design of new public buildings

Remember

social benefit = private benefit + external benefit.

Key terms

Social benefit: the benefit to society consisting of private benefits and external benefits.

Activities

7   List all the external benefits that an airline creates.

8   Discuss the case for allowing a major airport to expand in terms of the social costs and benefits created from the expansion.

What can governments do about externalities?

The following two examples illustrate how governments might intervene:

- Car drivers don't pay for the negative externalities caused by exhaust fumes. Taxes placed on petrol attempt to reduce this external cost as the higher price for petrol should mean that fewer car journeys take place.
- Society benefits from a well-educated population because those educated usually earn more. Therefore, the UK government gives assistance to encourage more people to attend university, for example, by giving grants.

AQA Examiner's tip

The value of externalities is almost impossible to accurately measure – don't assume that they can be calculated.

Economic cycle

What is the economic cycle?

In the UK, average economic growth is approximately 2.5 per cent per year. However, the actual rate of growth varies over time.

The economic cycle shows how economies grow at different rates and this pattern will be repeated in a cyclical (i.e. repeated) manner. The stages of the economic cycle are as follows:

- boom
- recession
- slump
- recovery.

The definition of what a recession is can vary between countries. In the UK a recession only occurs when there is negative economic growth for two consecutive quarters of the year, but other countries define this differently.

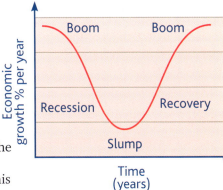

Economic cycle

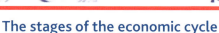

The stages of the economic cycle

Boom

Economic growth will be above average. Consumer spending is likely to be high and rising as people feel confident and are more likely to borrow money to finance more spending. Unemployment is likely to be falling or low. Investment will rise as businesses seek to expand. There is likely to be upward pressure on prices because of the increased demand for goods and the resources to produce those goods (labour and capital). As a result, inflation will start to rise.

D *The stages of the economic cycle*

Stage of economic cycle	Recession	Slump	Recovery	Boom
Rate of economic growth	Below average and falling	Low and possibly negative	Low but rising	Above average and possibly high

Recession

Economic growth will start to fall below the average growth rate, although the rate of economic growth will still be positive (i.e. national income will still be rising, but at a lower rate). Consumer spending will slow down (it may still be rising but at a slower rate of growth) and unemployment will start to rise.

Business investment is likely to fall from its peak as managers feel less confident about future prospects. Inflation is likely to fall from its peak, but prices will still be rising. Imports may start to decline as consumer spending slows (consumers will cut back on spending which means less spending on imported goods).

As the recession continues and worsens it could turn into a slump.

E *Recession or slump?*

Slump

In a slump, growth will be low or negative.

Consumer spending will be low and could actually be falling where consumer spending is lower than in earlier time periods. This is likely to be because consumers feel pessimistic and insecure about their jobs, and the chances of keeping their jobs in the future.

F *In a slump, the economy shrinks*

Inflation is likely to be low and/or falling in a slump, as businesses attempt to encourage more spending by keeping prices unchanged or even cutting them. In some slumps prices may even begin to fall over time (falling prices are known as deflation). With low consumer spending, imports are likely to be low in growth or even falling – which could mean that the trade section of the balance of payments moves into surplus, where exports exceed imports.

Recovery

Economic growth will start to rise towards the average level again. If economic growth has been negative, it will start to reach positive rates again. Confidence will return to customers and businesses. Consumer spending will start to rise again and businesses will begin investing again. Unemployment is likely to stop rising and may even begin to fall, although the level of unemployment may still be high. Inflation will stop falling.

G The property market is considered a good indicator of the 'green shoots' of recovery – when more houses are bought and sold

Case study

Economic growth in the UK

The following chart shows recent UK economic growth.

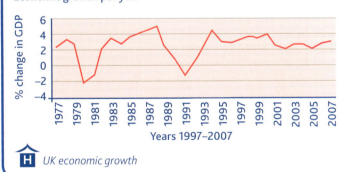

H UK economic growth

Activities

9 State which stage of the economic cycle the UK economy was in for the following years:

a 1989   b 1979   c 1991   d 1994.

10 In 1987–8, the UK economy entered the boom stage of the economic cycle. Explain the likely features of economic performance for this period.

AQA Examiner's tip

Don't presume that the stages of the economic cycle are of the same length. The length of stages varies in each cycle.

Government economic policy

Government revenue and expenditure

The government contributes greatly to economic growth through its own expenditure. To finance this spending, the government will raise money through **taxation**.

Indirect taxes

Indirect taxes are taxes placed on expenditure. They are added on to the selling price of a product. In the UK, valued added tax (VAT) is levied on most goods and services at the rate of 15 per cent (though this is set to rise by 2010). Other indirect taxes include customs duties (taxes placed on imported goods) and excise duties (taxes placed on specific goods such as petrol, alcohol and tobacco).

Direct taxes

Direct taxes are those placed on incomes earned by individuals. Income tax is the main direct tax levied by the government. In the UK, there are two rates of taxation: the basic rate of 20 per cent and the higher rate of 40 per cent of income.

National insurance is another tax on income. Businesses also pay national insurance contributions for every worker they employ. Other direct taxes include **corporation tax,** which is paid by limited companies on the profits they have made.

Other taxes

- Stamp duty is placed on the purchase price of a house at varying rates.
- Council tax is charged on each house in the country and varies according to the value of the property.
- Inheritance tax is paid on any inheritance earned when an estate (the total wealth of an individual) passes on to someone else when the individual dies.

Government expenditure

There are various categories on which the government spends its revenue. The highest areas are as follows:

Social protection

This will include welfare payments (e.g. unemployment benefits) paid to those in need. Qualification for some benefits is not automatic (e.g. for the Jobseeker's Allowance, an applicant must prove that they are actively seeking work). Some welfare payments are based on a person's financial circumstances (i.e. people qualify if they have insufficient savings). Others are paid regardless of status (e.g. child benefits are paid to all regardless of the family income).

A *Each house incurs a council tax*

Health

Health spending is the second largest component of government expenditure. The National Health Service (NHS) provides most health care freely to anyone who wants treatment. Not all governments share the idea of free universal health care. As the UK population is ageing, the demands on the NHS are likely to rise for the future.

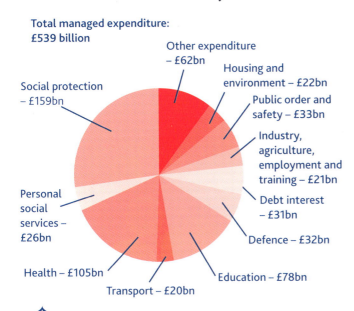

Total managed expenditure: £539 billion

Other expenditure – £62bn
Housing and environment – £22bn
Public order and safety – £33bn
Industry, agriculture, employment and training – £21bn
Debt interest – £31bn
Defence – £32bn
Education – £78bn
Transport – £20bn
Health – £105bn
Personal social services – £26bn
Social protection – £159bn

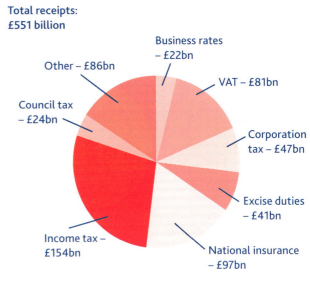

Total receipts: £551 billion

Business rates – £22bn
Other – £86bn
VAT – £81bn
Council tax – £24bn
Corporation tax – £47bn
Income tax – £154bn
Excise duties – £41bn
National insurance – £97bn

Source: www.statistics.gov.uk

B *UK Government revenue and expenditure for 2007*

▉ Fiscal policy

What is fiscal policy?

Governments spend large amounts in the economy. Therefore changes in **government expenditure** have a major impact on economic performance and the government's ability to reach its economic objectives.

This high expenditure means that taxes are also a significant proportion of both expenditure and income. Changes in taxation have a significant effect on the performance of the economy.

Fiscal policy refers to the choices and decisions made for government spending and the taxation that will go towards financing the expenditure.

The effects of fiscal policy

Changes in the level of government spending, and changes in the level of taxation, will affect each of the government's economic objectives.

Key terms

Government expenditure: money spent by the government on public services and welfare.

Fiscal policy: decisions made by the government for government expenditure and taxation.

Activity

2 Look up the details of the last UK budget from the HM Treasury website – what were the major tax changes?

∞links

www.hm-treasury.gov.uk

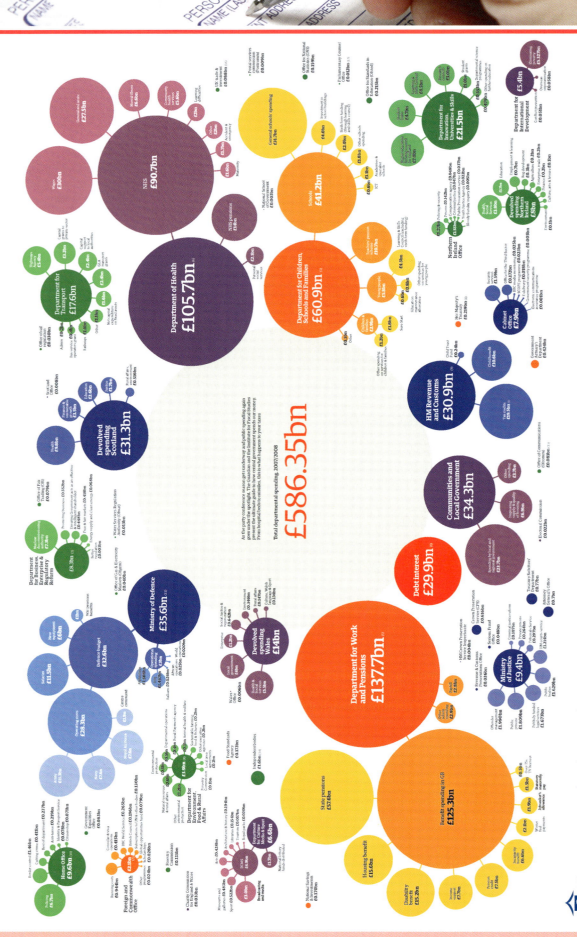

£586.35bn

At the party conference season gets underway and public spending again goes under the spotlight, The Guardian and the Institute for Fiscal Studies present the ultimate guide to how central government spends our money. From hospital beds to missiles, this is what happens to your taxes

Total departmental spending, 2007/2008

NHS £90.7bn
Department of Health £105.7bn
Department for Transport £17.6bn
Schools £41.2bn
General schools spending £31bn
Department for Children, Schools and Families £60.9bn
Department for Innovation, Universities & Skills £21.5bn
Department for International Development £5.4bn
Devolved spending Scotland £31.3bn
Devolved spending Northern Ireland £8bn
Northern Ireland Office
Cabinet Office £7.9bn
Her Majesty's Treasury
HM Revenue and Customs £30.9bn
Communities and Local Government £34.3bn
Debt interest £29.9bn
Department for Business, Enterprise & Regulatory Reform £8.3bn
Ministry of Defence £35.6bn
Devolved spending Wales £14bn
Department for Work and Pensions £137.7bn
Ministry of Justice £9.4bn
Home Office £9.6bn
Foreign and Commonwealth Office
Department for Environment, Food & Rural Affairs
Department for Culture, Media & Sport £6.6bn
State pensions £57.6bn
Benefit spending in GB £125.3bn

UK government spending: the 2007–8 budget. To see this graphic on screen go to:
http://image.guardian.co.uk/sys-files/Guardian/documents/2008/09/12/13.09.08.Public.spending.pdf

Inflation

Increases in government spending can lead to higher inflation. If spending in the economy is already rising, any extra government spending might contribute to higher inflation. If spending in the economy is generally low and/or falling, it is possible that any increases in government spending will not lead to higher inflation.

A reduction in taxation also encourages more expenditure. This is because consumers (and businesses if the tax reduction is on business profits) will now keep a higher proportion of any income earned. This may lead to higher consumer spending, which could push inflation higher. Therefore, governments may consider raising taxes to reduce upward pressure on inflation because higher taxes reduce people's ability to spend.

Economic growth

As the government contributes to a major proportion of overall spending, any changes in the level of spending will lead to changes in the level of economic growth. Higher government spending should encourage faster economic growth – a strategy used by many governments when facing either a slump or a recession.

Cuts in taxation may also lead to faster economic growth. Tax cuts mean consumers have higher disposable income, which normally encourages more consumer spending. This boosts economic growth.

Unemployment

Higher government spending is likely to reduce unemployment as higher spending creates more demand for output, meaning that more workers are required. Similarly, lower taxation encourages more spending and has the same effect. The opposite is also true. Higher taxation and lower government spending are both likely to contribute to rising unemployment.

Balance of payments

Higher government spending and lower taxation both lead to faster economic growth through higher overall spending. This is likely to conflict with the government's objective of achieving a balance on the current account. Higher growth means that more people are willing to spend, which leads to rising imports. However, there will be no positive effect on exports – these are affected by economic growth in other countries and therefore the balance of payments will decline.

■ Monetary policy

What is monetary policy?

The **Bank of England** is the UK's central bank. It is the centre of the UK's financial system, and is responsible for setting **monetary policy**. In the UK, monetary policy involves changes in **interest rates** that represent the cost of borrowing money. Interest rates are set monthly by the Bank of England and are used to control inflation and economic growth.

AQA Examiner's tip

When writing about the effects of change in government policy, it is better to use language suggesting the effects of the change are not entirely certain (i.e. use words like 'could' and 'may' rather than 'would' and 'will').

Key terms

Bank of England: the UK's central bank and responsible for issuing and controlling the money in the economy.

Monetary policy: policy to control the supply or cost of money.

Interest rate: the cost of borrowing and the reward for saving money.

Controlling inflation

One major cause of inflation is from spending in the economy rising too quickly. Interest-rate rises can help to slow down inflation caused by excessive spending. This will work as follows:

- Most house purchases are financed by mortgages. Interest payments on these mortgages will be paid monthly and depend on the level of interest rates. Higher interest rates means higher monthly repayments meaning households have less money available to spend. This should ease pressure on inflation.

- Many high-value purchases (e.g. new cars) are financed on credit – where consumers buy now but pay later. Higher interest rates discourage this sort of purchase as payments for the product (including higher interest charges) increase. This also eases pressure on inflation.

- Higher interest rates encourage saving due to the higher interest on savings. Obviously, this leads to less spending in the economy.

- Since 1997, the Bank of England has been instructed to set interest rates each month to keep UK inflation low and stable at around 2 per cent.

Activities

4 By how much did interest rates fall between September 2007 and November 2008?

5 Outline the possible effects of the cuts in interest rates in 2008 on
a economic growth, and
b inflation.

UK interest rates

D *UK Interest rates: March 2006–November 2008*

Source: BBC website – www.bbc.co.uk

Controlling growth

Interest rate reductions should lead to higher spending and faster economic growth. The Bank of England will reduce interest rates if it feels that inflation is unlikely to rise but economic growth could be faster.

Higher spending and higher growth in the economy are likely to lead to reductions in unemployment as more spending means that more output is needed and more workers will be required to produce this output.

Activity

6 Explain why a rise in interest rates might actually lead to higher inflation in the short term.

Supply-side policies

What is the supply side?

Economic growth can be increased with more spending. However, if spending rises quicker than the rate at which output increases, then the higher spending leads to higher inflation. Therefore, it is important that an economy can produce more output over time. Policies to raise the rate of growth of output without boosting spending are known as **supply-side policies**. Successful supply-side policies allow economies to grow faster with fewer risks of inflation.

AQA Examiner's tip

When looking at the effects of changes in interest rates, don't forget that it will sometimes take over one year for the change to have its full effect.

Key terms

Supply-side policy: government policies to encourage the economy to increase its potential growth rate.

What are supply-side policies?

Supply-side policies are varied in nature and cover a wide range of different policies, as follows:

Education and training

Increasing the quality and the quantity of educational and training should make people more productive. This higher productivity should lead to higher national output. The UK government has implemented many policies over the last 20 years in order to achieve this goal, such as:

- education maintenance allowance (EMA) grants to encourage people to 'stay on' in education until they are 18
- expansion of university provision – the numbers attending university have increased significantly
- national vocational qualifications (NVQs) to encourage workers to undertake work-based training
- policies to encourage more long-term unemployed people to undertake training.

Competition

Encouraging **competition** between businesses should lead to higher output levels and lower prices because of the pressure between businesses to retain customers. Aid for small businesses will help them survive and compete with larger businesses.

During the 1980s and 1990s, many UK firms were transferred from the public sector to the private sector (privatisation) in order to create more competition.

Markets have been deregulated. Deregulation means removing legal restrictions that restrict businesses. It allows new businesses to enter the market creating competition. For example, the UK firm British Telecom (BT) was first privatised in the 1980s and gradually the market was deregulated to allow more competition which led to improved services and lower prices.

Labour market policies

Decreasing direct taxes provides workers with incentives to rejoin the workforce, and also for firms to recruit more workers. Traditionally, trade unions resisted the introduction of labour-saving technology and also used their power to push for higher wages. A reduction in trade union power has encouraged firms to recruit more workers.

Evaluation of supply-side policies

These policies have been put into place over the last 30 years. However, some of these policies take many years to have their full effect. Supply-side policies have been controversial as they often reduce the power of workers in the workplace. However, UK unemployment has generally been lower than other members of the EU countries where supply-side policies have not been as widespread.

E *Investment in training young people makes the economy more productive*

Key terms

Competition policy: policies designed to increase competition in a market.

AQA Examiner's tip

Supply-side policies are meant to be used with fiscal and monetary policy – not instead of them.

4.6 The role of the European Union (EU)

Effects of membership of the EU

History of the EU

The European Union (EU) is a collection of 27 European nations that cooperate together on economic and political issues. The EU began in the 1950s as an agreement between six countries to engage in free trade for certain products. Countries joined this organisation at various stages (the UK joined in 1973).

The role of the EU has also developed into much more than a free-trade area, as closer links are made and cooperation takes place. Today, the EU is a large organisation that contains almost 500 million people, has its own parliament and sets rules and regulations across each member country.

Objectives

Understand what the EU represents.

Understand the arguments for and against EU membership.

Understand the case for having a single currency.

Understand the reasons for the UK's non-membership of the euro.

Understand how the EU has enlarged over recent years.

A The membership of the European Union

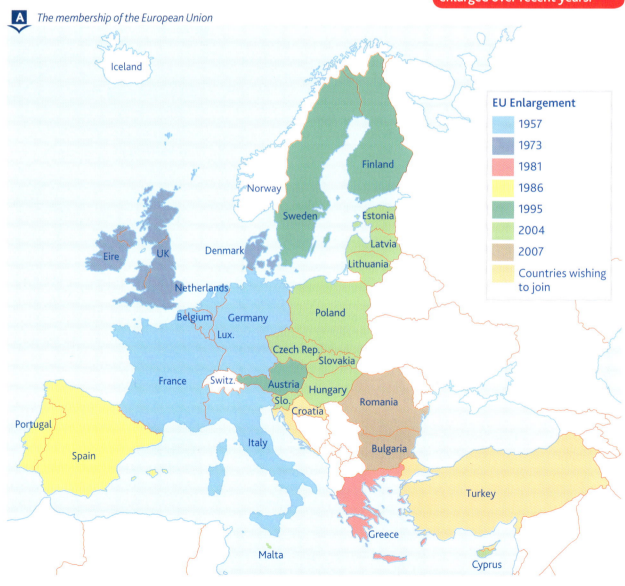

EU Enlargement

- 1957
- 1973
- 1981
- 1986
- 1995
- 2004
- 2007
- Countries wishing to join

Free trade

One of the main attractions of being an EU member is that it allows free trade between EU countries. This means that buying and selling goods between countries should be as easy as buying and selling within one country. If free trade exists, there can be no tariffs on goods or services. Tariffs are a tax placed on imports designed to discourage people from buying imports and to encourage people to buy the home-produced goods instead.

In the EU, there is a common external tariff placed on goods coming into the EU from outside. This tariff is the same in every EU country. The purpose of the common external tariff is to discourage EU citizens from buying goods from outside the EU and to encourage the purchase of EU goods instead.

Protectionism

The common external tariff is a form of protectionism. This is where imports are discouraged so as to promote the home-produced goods instead. Therefore, the industries producing these goods are protected from the effects of foreign competition from outside the EU.

Although protectionism may help industries to survive because the threat of foreign competition is reduced, protectionism limits the choice of consumers who cannot buy imported products without paying a higher price through the tariffs placed on the goods. If tariffs are used by a country, then there is a danger that the industries protected will never become efficient as they have no threat of competition to drive them to improve performance.

Single European market

Since 1993, the EU has operated a single European market. This incorporates free trade between EU members but also has some additional features:

- Free movement of workers – getting a job in another country should be no more difficult than getting a job in the worker's home country.
- Free movement of capital – money should be able to move freely between countries in the EU with no barriers to transfers.
- Common product standards – all goods provided across the EU should conform to the same health and safety standards.

B *There are many economic benefits to joining the EU*

UK membership of the EU

The UK joined the EU (then known as the European Economic Community) back in 1973. Membership of the EU has been subject to debate and, while none of the main political parties recommend withdrawal, there are many people who feel that the drawbacks are more significant. Many of the benefits and drawbacks that arise from EU membership are listed overleaf.

Activity

1 Analyse the possible effects of the expansion of the EU in 2004 on the UK economy.

C *The benefits of EU membership – ease of trade enables a German market to trade on a city street in the UK*

Benefits of EU membership

- Greater choice for consumers – being an EU member means that consumers have access to a wider range of goods, which should be available without having to pay tariffs.

- Larger market for businesses – opportunities for businesses to expand will be greater if a country is a member of the EU. The population of the EU is around 500 million – ten times more than the UK. This allows businesses the chance to target a greater number of consumers and, potentially, become more efficient through economies of scale.

- Higher incomes – free trade should benefit all members of the free-trade area. This is because countries can specialise in the production of goods they are more skilled at producing and can then trade these with each other.

- Political influence – joining the EU means that a country is granted various powers to influence policy. Remaining outside the EU means that the country would not have power in guiding any future policy decisions of the EU.

Drawbacks of EU membership

- Competition for UK firms – UK firms have to compete with other EU firms. If these EU firms are from countries where costs are significantly lower (e.g. cheap wages), it may be very hard for the UK firms to compete successfully.

- Lack of freedom on product standards – UK businesses have to ensure that products conform to EU health and safety standards. This may cost both money and time. If the UK left the EU, it would not have to fulfil these requirements.

- Common agricultural policy – the UK contributes money for the EU's common agricultural policy (CAP). This is a system whereby agricultural prices are guaranteed and this means that farmers can expect a guaranteed income for their output. This benefits countries where the agricultural industry is inefficient. However, in countries like the UK, farmers lose out. UK farmers are generally far more efficient than other EU members but cannot offer their products for a lower price because of the CAP.

The euro €

Background

The single European currency (the euro) was planned for many years before it was finally launched. Exchange rate systems were set up in the 1970s and 1980s as the step towards a **common** (single) **currency**. However, in 1992 a treaty was signed that paved the way for full monetary union through the creation of the euro. Although the euro was launched in 1999, it was three years before the notes and coins were circulated. Twelve countries of the EU joined in the first wave, with the UK, Sweden and Denmark opting out. By January 2009, there were 16 countries (the '**eurozone**') using the euro as their currency.

Reasons for joining the euro

Reduced transactions costs

There are no costs of converting one currency into another. If businesses outside the euro engage in foreign trade on a frequent basis, they will incur high costs in currency conversion.

Uncompetitive exports

With separate currencies, it is possible for a country to have a particular exchange rate level where it is hard for businesses to compete with businesses in other countries. This makes it hard for businesses to export products to the other countries. A single currency should reduce the problems of having uncompetitive exports.

Ease of price comparisons

Consumers will find it easier to compare prices of goods sold by different countries. Businesses will not be able to charge different prices in different countries as easily as when separate currencies existed.

Greater economies of scale

Being in the eurozone has encouraged greater trade with other countries in the eurozone. This has allowed firms to expand. These firms will benefit from increased efficiency – known as economies of scale.

Reasons against joining the euro

Costs of preparation

Joining the euro requires a large amount of expenditure in switching from the old currency. Money needs to be spent training staff dealing with money about the switchover, and the general population will need to be educated in how the new currency will work.

Loss of control over interest rates

The interest rate for the euro is set by the European Central Bank (ECB). This means that any one country can no longer set its own interest rate at the level it would like for its own economy. Therefore, joining the euro means giving control of monetary policy to the ECB.

Key terms

Common currency: where two or more countries share the same currency.

Eurozone: the countries that have the euro as their currency.

Activity

2 Which countries have the euro as their national currency?

D *Which countries use the euro?*

E *The European Central Bank in Strasbourg*

∞ links

www.euro.gov.uk

Use of exchange rate

Allowing the exchange rate to fall in value is a way of boosting economic growth because it leads to a country's exports being more desirable in foreign countries as they appear cheaper. This is not possible in a single currency.

Why the UK is not a member of the euro

The UK government has promised that the general public will be given a vote on joining the euro at some point in the future. Until then, the UK will remain outside the eurozone.

It is believed that the UK economy and those economies in the euro are too different for the UK to be a successful member. For instance, the UK often needs interest rates at a level different to those set by the ECB.

The UK population is less pro-European than most other EU nations. It is highly unlikely that the majority would vote to join in the near future.

■ EU enlargement

Recent enlargement

Since 2004, twelve more countries have joined the EU. This **enlargement** has almost doubled the number of countries within the EU. Many of these new members are countries from **Eastern** and Central **Europe**.

Effects of expansion

The inclusion of Eastern European countries in the EU is likely to have the following effects on existing EU members.

Cheaper labour costs

The Eastern European countries joining the EU are not as wealthy as the existing members. This means that wages are lower and therefore labour costs will be lower. This may provide a cost-saving advantage for Western European firms that operate in other countries.

Greater competition

The new members of the EU will not be subject to the common external tariff. This means that Western European businesses will face greater competition from firms within the Eastern European countries.

More choice for consumers

Not having the common external tariff imposed on imports from these new members of the EU will make it easier and cheaper for UK consumers to buy goods from these countries.

The future of the EU

It is likely that there will eventually be more countries joining the EU. Several countries have already begun negotiations to join. The EU border may shift further eastwards as enlargement continues. There are also likely to be new members from the former Yugoslavia (a country which split into several smaller countries).

€/£

F Pound/euro exchange rate 2007–8

Source: www.economist.com

Activity

The £ : € exchange rate

3 Looking at the diagram **F** of the £ : € exchange rate, explain the likely effect on the UK economy of the change since 2007.

Key terms

Enlargement: bringing new member countries into the EU.

Eastern Europe: countries geographically located towards the East of Europe, several of which are recent members of the EU or are in negotiations to join.

Activities

4 What would be the effects of more countries joining the EU on the UK government's ability to meet its economic objectives?

5 Which countries are currently in negotiation for EU membership?

∞ links

EU commission page on enlargement
http://ec.europa.eu/enlargement/index_en.htm

Chapter summary

By now you should have a clear understanding of:

✔ what the government economic objectives are and how they are measured

✔ why economic growth is important and the drawbacks of growth

✔ what the welfare state is and what the alternatives are

✔ what the different types of economic system are

✔ how externalities arise and other ways in which markets can fail

✔ what the features of the economic cycle are

✔ what areas the government spends money on and how this is financed

✔ how monetary, fiscal and supply-side policies are used to control the economy

✔ what the consequences of EU membership are and how it will be affected by enlargement

✔ the arguments for and against joining the euro.

Revision quiz

1 List four economic objectives of the government.

2 Name the two methods used to measure UK inflation.

3 How is the unemployment rate calculated?

4 Explain two benefits and two drawbacks of economic growth.

5 Define social cost and give three examples of negative externalities.

6 Define external benefit and give two examples.

7 State the four stages of the economic cycle.

8 Explain how indirect and direct taxes are used to collect revenue for the government.

9 Analyse the effects of an interest-rate reduction on the UK economy.

10 Analyse the effects of a rise in income taxes on consumer spending.

11 Describe how supply-side policies are used in the UK.

12 What are the benefits for the UK remaining a member of the EU?

13 Discuss the case for joining the euro.

■ Topics for research

Two topics will be chosen from study each year for you to study in more detail. One of the topics will be based on local, UK or EU issues and the other will relate to the global economy. The topics can change each year, but it is likely that they will initially be chosen from the following list:

- **environmental issues**: causes, consequences and solutions
- **global warming** and its effect on different economies and societies
- **globalisation**: the benefits and drawbacks from an economic viewpoint and ethical issues with the development of the world economy
- **developing economies**: India and China – issues of growth and the impact on developed countries
- **underdevelopment**: its causes and cures, focusing on least developed economies, e.g. sub-Saharan Africa
- **dominant firms**: impact on consumers and producers plus issues of control and regulation
- **poverty**: disparities in living standards and the ethical issues that arise from the implications of choice for society.

These topics should be researched in order to gain an understanding of the subject matter in more detail so that you can analyse and evaluate the issues that the topic raises.

Much of this research can be done using the internet, which can supply extensive information relating to each of these topics. However, you should be careful and try to be selective in the information that you collect. Try to stick to repeatable websites that are likely to give you accurate, objective information. Some useful websites that you can use are:

http://news.bbc.co.uk/   www.economist.com/
www.timesonline.co.uk   www.ft.com
www.hm-treasury.gov.uk/   www.guardian.co.uk/
http://www.ukinvest.gov.uk/   www.bankofengland.co.uk/
www.oecd.org   www.statistics.gov.uk/

Try to keep a file or folder containing interesting articles that you find during your research. Collect a range of articles and information with a variety of data – and make sure that you understand the data that you collect. The articles and data that you collect do not have to be complicated, so be wary of those that come from higher education institution websites. In addition, try to ensure that you collect information from the local area. This could be in the form of searching through local newspapers or approaching organisations in your own area.

Examination-style questions

The Unit 11 examination will assess the theory, knowledge and concepts covered in Chapters 1, 2 and 3; the Unit 12 examination will cover the content you have studied in Chapter 4, plus a question on each of the two topics you have researched for Current Economic Issues. For this examination there will be three questions in total. The questions on current economic issues will require you to use the content of the entire GCSE Economics course.

Unit 11-style questions

1   Amrita finished veterinary college two years ago, and has been employed as a vet ever since. She earns a good salary for a 26-year-old and despite all the expenses of setting up home has been able to save for a deposit to buy a house. Added to a small inheritance she now has £20000 in savings.

Because she does so much travelling to clients, she feels she also needs to buy a new van for business use. Prices of vans have recently begun to fall and intense competition between van dealers has meant that Amrita thinks it is now a good time to buy the van.

Her financial adviser has also suggested she takes out a private pension plan, which would pay her an income when she retires. Amrita thinks that getting a new car is priority at the moment - after all, she is only 26!

   (a)   **(i)**   What is meant by the term 'savings'?   *(2 marks)*

   (ii)   define the term 'opportunity cost' and give one example of an opportunity cost to Paula of using her savings to buy her new car   *(3 marks)*

   (b)   Any surplus money left over after the van is purchased could be saved in an ISA. Outline **three** features of an ISA.   *(3 marks)*

   (c)   Explain **three** possible ways, other than price, in which van dealers might compete with each other.   *(6 marks)*

   (d)   Paula thinks that at 26 a new van is her priority rather than saving for a pension. Would you advise Paula to save for her pension or to buy a new car? Explain your answer.   *(12 marks)*

2   Helen Clews is currently deciding what to do for her future job. She has just finished her degree at her local university. Her dream career is to work as a journalist on one of the national newspapers. Her university degree is in English Literature. However, there are no current vacancies at present. There are jobs on local newspapers available but these will require Helen to move to a new city away from her boyfriend. There are rumours amongst internet chat rooms that the national newspapers are unlikely to make any major recruitment for 12 months, but that they will begin to recruit people with relevant experience at that time.

Helen's alternative to moving away is to take on temporary work at the local newspaper. This will not pay as well, but it will be in the local area. The other alternative is for Helen to sign on as unemployed – this may give Helen time to complete some sample articles that she could send with her CV and application.

   (a)   State **three** ways in which Helen may be paid if she works for the local newspaper.   *(2 marks)*

   (b)   Explain the difference between gross and net pay.   *(2 marks)*

   (c)   Analyse the factors which determine how many journalists a national newspaper would employ.   *(6 marks)*

   (d)   Explain **two** reasons why a journalist might receive higher wages at a national as opposed to a local newspaper.   *(4 marks)*

   (e)   Helen thinks that moving away from her local town would be too difficult. Would you advise Helen to stay or move away to work on one of the local newspapers elsewhere?   *(12 marks)*

3   Estelle has set up a mobile catering company. Her friend Rob, who recently came over from Australia, helped her get it established. They are keen to support Fairtrade products and sell items with minimal environmental impact. She will therefore try and buy as few products from abroad as possible. In order for her to be able to provide a truly flexible service however, she needs to import some specialist food cabinets from Germany.

The company has been very successful so far, but profit margins are low. Estelle thinks she will need two full-time members of staff, but is not in a position to pay high wages. However, in the local labour market she feels that there is not enough skilled labour available .

The fall in the exchange rate over the last year has also been an issue. The exchange rate has fallen from £1 : €1.4 to £1 : €1.2.

(a)   Explain **two** reasons why employing migrant labour might provide a solution to Estelle's recruitment problems.   *(6 marks)*

(b)   The German equipment she plans to buy costs €4000.

    (i)   Calculate how much the machinery would cost in pounds at £1: €1.2.   *(2 marks)*

    (ii)   Explain the likely impact this change in the exchange rate could have on the number of imports the UK buys from Germany each year.   *(3 marks)*

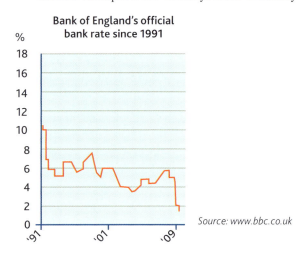

Source: www.bbc.co.uk

(c)   Discuss how the pound falling by a significant amount might affect Estelle's business.   *(12 marks)*

Unit 12-style questions

4   Interest rates, set by the Bank of England, were cut rapidly in Autumn 2008 from 5% and fell to their lowest ever level in January 2009 of 1.5%.

(a)   (i)   What is meant by the term 'interest rate'?   *(2 marks)*

    (ii)   Explain **three** ways in which a large cut in interest rates might affect economic growth.   *(6 marks)*

(b)   (i)   Interest rates are often increased to reduce the rate of inflation. Explain **two** reasons why the government would want to reduce inflation.   *(4 marks)*

    (ii)   Interest rate reduction can help reduce unemployment. Discus the alternative methods a government can use to reduce unemployment.   *(12 marks)*

5   Read the following article and study the charts that follow.

Official advisers to the UK government have demanded that Britain slash greenhouse gases by a fifth of current levels by 2020 – the toughest target so far. The Committee on Climate Change has said that a cut of 21 per cent on 2005 levels is needed for the UK to play its fair share in combating dangerous climate change.

This has major implications for the UK's energy policy. The report says that fuel will inevitably become more expensive to achieve the carbon targets. But it also says that the government will need to compensate poor households rather than trying to keep prices down.

The report has been generally welcomed by environmentalists, but they are angry that the committee has not set any specific targets for aviation – the fastest-growing source of emissions.

The committee has put aviation into the overall carbon budget but exempted it from specific targets until disputes over responsibility for international aviation emissions have been resolved.

Lord Turner, the committee chairman, said that the cuts could be achieved without compromising our lifestyles or economy: 'The reductions can be achieved at very low cost (an estimated 1% loss of GDP growth in 2020). The cost of not achieving the reductions at a national and global level will be far greater.'

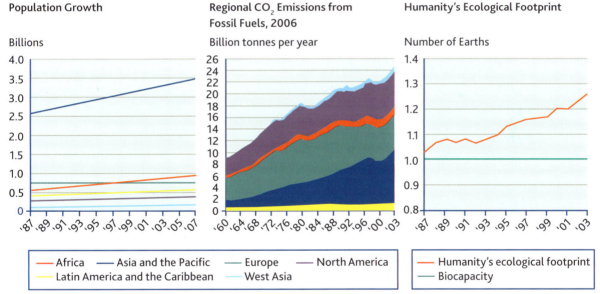

Population Growth

Billions

Regional CO$_2$ Emissions from Fossil Fuels, 2006

Billion tonnes per year

Humanity's Ecological Footprint

Number of Earths

Africa — Asia and the Pacific — Europe — North America
Latin America and the Caribbean — West Asia

Humanity's ecological footprint
Biocapacity

Source: www.bbc.co.uk

(a) Using the charts given, state which region has seen the greatest percentage rise in CO$_2$ emissions from fossil fuels over the period shown.   (*1 mark*)

(b) Approximately what is the total quantity of CO$_2$ emissions from fossil fuels that originate from Europe in 2003?   (*1 mark*)

(c) Explain why 'fuel will inevitably become more expensive' if the UK government is to achieve its carbon emission targets.   (*3 marks*)

(d) Explain the effects on the aviation industry of increasing the taxes on air travel.   (*6 marks*)

(e) Do you think that these types of taxes (on air travel) would benefit the UK economy? Justify your view.   (*12 marks*)

Glossary

A

Absolute poverty: those with incomes lower than the level needed for necessities.

Annual Equivalent Rate (AER): a figure quoted in savings advertisements to help people compare one savings product with another.

Annual Percentage Rate (APR): the interest rate published on loans to help compare their true costs.

B

Balance of payments: a record of the value of a country's exports, imports and financial transactions with the rest of the world over the year.

Bank of England: the UK's central bank and responsible for issuing and controlling the money in the economy.

Bank/building society savings account: an account for which the main objective is to gain interest and keep money safe.

Bankers' Automated Clearing Service (BACS): automatic transfer of funds between bank accounts (e.g. employer's to employee's).

Basic economic problem: resources are limited but 'needs' and 'wants' are infinite.

Benefits: (1) regular payments from a government to support people in need.

Benefits: (2) the advantages of a particular choice.

Borrowing/debt/credit: getting money from a lender that must be repaid in the future (e.g. a mortgage).

Boycott: to stop buying or using a product as a protest, to force a company to do, or stop doing, a particular action.

Budget: a financial plan of future income and spending.

C

Carbon footprint: the total greenhouse gas (CO_2 equivalent) emissions caused by an individual, event, organisation or product or good traded by the UK.

Choice: deciding between different options because our resources are limited.

Commission: payment made to workers for achieving a certain target (e.g. sales levels).

Common currency: where two or more currencies share the same currency.

Competition: the process of trying to beat others (e.g. trying to gain more customers).

Competition policy: policies designed to increase competition in a market.

Consumer empowerment: consumers demonstrating their needs, wants and demands through their purchase decisions in the marketplace.

Corporation tax: tax on the profits of limited companies.

Costs: the expenses and drawbacks of a particular choice.

D

Debt: the amount still owing from funds borrowed.

Debt management: taking the help of an expert to solve a debt problem.

Debt management plan: a structured repayment plan.

Demand: the quantity of a good or service that consumers will purchase at a particular price.

Demerit goods: goods that are over-consumed by society.

Direct taxes: taxes on incomes (e.g. income tax).

E

Eastern Europe: countries geographically located towards the East of Europe, several of which are recent members of the EU or are in negotiations to join.

Economic growth: the percentage change in national income measured over time.

Economic objectives: economic goals.

Emigration: leaving one's native country or region to settle in another.

Enlargement: the process of admitting new members to the EU.

Equality: where incomes are distributed more equally.

Ethical lending policy: a statement that loans will only be made to businesses that act in a socially responsible manner.

Ethics: the 'rights' and 'wrongs' of an issue.

Eurozone: the countries that have the euro as their currency.

Exchange rates: the rate at which one currency exchanges for another.

Expenses: payments given to workers to compensate for any expenditure necessary to complete their work.

Exports: goods and services sold to another country.

Externalities: the additional costs or benefits beyond private ones imposed on society that arises out of a production or consumption decision.

F

Factors affecting demand: things that cause consumers to buy more or less of a product at a given price.

Factors affecting sales of exports and imports: things that influence consumers to buy imports/exports, other than price.

Factors affecting supply: things that cause suppliers to offer more or less of a good or service at a particular price.

Financial adviser: a professional offering financial advice.

Financial planning: a process for ensuring that financial goals are met.

Fiscal policy: decisions made by the government for government expenditure and taxation.

Flexible working: workers who are more adaptable in time, location or manner of work completed (e.g. home working).

Foreign direct investment: when a business from one country builds a factory in another.

Free market economy: a system where all economic decisions are taken by private individuals and businesses.

Full-time: a worker who works the maximum number of hours required in the normal working week for a particular job.

G

Gaining employment: being offered and accepting a paid job.

Globalisation: the process of increasing international trade and economic interdependence between countries.

Government expenditure: money spent by the government on public services and welfare.

Government securities: stocks, bonds and bills of exchange issued by a government to raise the funds.

Gross Domestic Product (GDP): total value of goods and services produced by an economy in one year.

Gross pay: a worker's pay before any deductions are made.

I

Immigration: migration into a country.

Imports: goods and services bought from another country.

Income: total money received from a person's wages/salary, interest and dividends.

Income tax: a tax calculated as a percentage of a worker's income.

Information and Communication Technology (ICT): the use of electronic and computer technology.

Interest rates: an annual rate which is charged to borrowers or paid to savers.

Interest taxes: taxes on expenditure (e.g. VAT).

ISA: individual Savings Account on which interest is tax free.

L

Labour costs: costs of employing workers (e.g., wages, salaries, taxes on labour) and also training and recruitment costs.

Leaving school, college/ university: when a person ceases to be in full-time education and looks for employment.

Loan: amount of money borrowed.

M

Market failure: a failure of the market to allocate resources efficiently.

Market price: the price that buyers and sellers agree on for a particular good or service.

Markets: a market exists whenever buyers and sellers come together.

Merit goods: goods that are under-consumed by society.

Migration: the movement of people from one country or region to another.

Mixed economy: a system that is partly a free-market economy but also has government involvement in economic decisions.

MNC: multinational corporation.

Mobility of labour: the ability of workers to change between jobs.

Monetary policy: policy to control the supply or cost of money.

Motivation: the reason that somebody does something.

N

National insurance (NI): a tax paid by workers which entitles the payee to qualify for benefits when and if necessary.

Need and want: needs are essential to our lives but wants are things we could easily survive without.

Net pay: pay after all deductions have been made.

O

Open economy: one that trades with other countries.

Opportunity cost: something given up when we make a choice.

Overtime payment: higher rate of pay for work in excess of normal working hours.

P

P45: a document provided by an employer when a worker leaves the organisation.

P60: a document provided by an employer on a yearly basis showing total pay and deductions for the year.

Part-time: this refers to a worker who only works a fraction of the working week of a full-time employee.

Pension contributions: a deduction from a worker's pay that is meant to contribute to a future retirement pension.

Pensions: a benefit paid as of right to those of retirement age who have paid the minimum National Insurance contributions.

Post Office card account: savings or current account offered by the Post Office..

Private benefit: the benefit to private businesses or individuals.

Private cost: the cost to private businesses or individuals.

Promotion: a new higher-paid job role involving greater responsibility and skill.

Public goods: goods that display the following two characteristics: consumption of them doesn't prevent others consuming them; once they are provided, people cannot be prevented from consuming them.

R

Relative poverty: those on low incomes relative to the country's average.

Resources: the land, labour, capital and enterprise used to produce goods and services.

Retirement: when we cease to do paid employment.

Reward: the return received for taking risks.

Risk: the chance that something may not succeed and its consequence.

S

Salary: pay stated as a yearly total.

Savings: putting money aside for later use.

Scarcity: resources are limited compared with our 'needs' and 'wants'.

Seasonal employment: work that is only required during a particular period of a year (e.g. some agricultural work).

Shares: certificate representing a unit of ownership in a company.

Shift work: work patterns that do not follow standard working hours.

Social benefit: the benefit to society consisting of private benefits and external benefits.

Social cost: the cost to society of an action consisting of private costs and external costs.

Social, moral or ethical dilemma: a problem with no absolute right or wrong solution.

Specialisation: where each worker concentrates on only one small aspect of the entire production process.

Stock market: the place where stocks, shares and bonds are traded.

Supply: the quantity of a good or service that businesses will offer for sale at a particular price.

Supply-side policy: government policies to encourage the economy to increase its potential growth rate.

T

Taxation: money collected by the government to finance its expenditure.

Tax allowances: sums deducted from total income before income tax is calculated.

Tax code: workers have different tax codes which relate to the different amount of tax-free allowance each worker has.

Tax credit: a state benefit paid to employees through the tax system, which acts like a negative tax.

Taxes: a fee levied by a government on a product, income, or activity.

Temporary employment: work that will only last for a specific period of time (usually a number of weeks or months).

Term of a loan: the length of time over which the loan can be repaid.

U

Unemployment: when an individual without a job is seeking paid employment or is able to work.

Unit trusts: a pooled investment fund usually in shares-based investments.

Wage: pay calculated on an hourly rate, multiplied by the hours worked.

Welfare state: financial or practical help for those who need the most support.

Index

Key terms and their page numbers are in blue